D0464098

A Consumer's Guide to the Apocalypse

Why There Is No Cultural War in America and Why We Will Perish Nonetheless

Eduardo Velásquez

ISI Books
Wilmington, Delaware
2007

Velásquez, Eduardo.
 A consumer's guide to the apocalypse / Eduardo Velásquez. — 1st ed.
 — Wilmington, DE : ISI Books, 2007.

   p. ; cm.

   ISBN-13: 978-1-933859-28-6
   ISBN-10: 1-933859-28-8

   1. Popular culture—United States. 2. United States—Civilization—
 1970–. 3. Philosophy, Modern—21st century. I. Title.

E169.12 .V45 2007   2007923890
973.93—dc22   0707

"News of the Soul's Death Greatly Exaggerated" originally appeared in *Shenandoah: The Washington and Lee University Review* 57, no. 1 (Spring 2007). It is reprinted here with the permission of the editor. "Knowledge of Ignorance" was originally published in *Perspectives on Political Science* 35, no. 3 (Summer 2006) and is reprinted by permission. Both essays have been revised for publication here. "Alpha and Omega" was first published in revised form in *Love and Friendship*, edited by Eduardo Velásquez, and is reprinted here by permission of the Rowman & Littlefield Publishing Group.

Book design by Kara Beer

Published in the United States by:

 ISI Books
 Intercollegiate Studies Institute
 Post Office Box 4431
 Wilmington, DE 19807-0431
 www.isibooks.org

forever Andrea, Diego, and Eliana

There is fiction in the space between
You and everybody
Give us all what we need
Give us one more sad sordid story
But in the fiction of the space between
Sometimes a lie is the best thing
Sometimes a lie is the best thing

— from Tracy Chapman, "Telling Stories"

A Primer for Annihilation

(Introduction)

ix

Part One: Science

News of the Soul's Death Greatly Exaggerated
(on Tom Wolfe's *I Am Charlotte Simmons*)
3

Knowledge of Ignorance
(on Michael Frayn's *Copenhagen*)
31

Beyond the Edge of Reason
(on Coldplay)
57

Part Two: Theology

Crown of Thorns
(on Dave Matthews)
77

Alpha and Omega
(on Chuck Palahniuk's *Fight Club*)
99

The Da Vinci Code
(on Tori Amos)
121

A New Genesis
(Conclusions)
147

Bibliographic Essay
153

Acknowledgments
159

Index
161

A Primer for Annihilation
(Introduction)

Nothing really matters to me. — Queen

What accounts for the popularity of ABC's hit series *Lost*, a story of marooned survivors on a mystical island haunted by dark forces, with mysterious computerized bunkers running underneath, at the same time that a biblical hue is cast over events? Have you wondered why the *New Battlestar Galactica* couches the futuristic quest of the last remaining humans in mythological language that harks back to the Greek gods? Why are the cylons (machines created by humans, some human enough to bear children) devout believers? Why are so many of the humans faithless cynics? Is the success of the *Matrix* trilogy a consequence of the marriage of myth, Bible, and science?

In other words, what explains the emergence of a litany of films and programs that interweave science and metaphysics at a time when the divide between secular and religious America has never seemed wider? Why these strange new mutations and conflations?

The trend is not limited to TV and the movies. Contemporary novelists have joined the chorus. The success of Margaret Atwood's scientific-metaphysical *The Handmaid's Tale* and *Oryx and Crake* is partly derived from her deft rethinking of cosmic questions in the context of nature transformed by science. She is not alone. Science-fiction writer Neal Stephenson returns to the Enlightenment (offering us a three-volume, almost 3,000-page fictitious history with the titles *Quicksilver, Confusion,* and *System World*) in order to revisit the connections between science and alchemy, religion and commerce. Why reconsider what the Enlightenment tore asunder? Fantasy writer Neil Gaiman's hugely successful *American Gods* situates a Jungian character named Shadow in a battle among Norse gods for America's soul. Does he see continuity between this book and his next, *Anansi Boys,* which he introduces with the epigraph "God is Dead. Meet the kids"? Is *American Gods* meant to be read as the tale of America after the death of the Christian God, and *Anansi Boys* as a depiction of an emerging soul weaned on the milk of a pantheistic or polytheistic America?

We see similar themes in popular music. Singer-songwriter Tori Amos has linked her album *Scarlet's Walk* to Gaiman's *American Gods.* Is the connection an appreciation of a mutual struggle for shared ends? Or take such songs from the Brit pop-rockers Coldplay as "The Scientist," "speed of sound," and "x and y." What do we make of their ruminations concerning the limitations of science, the nature of time, space, and darkness, and the tensions between the claims of reason and the claims of the heart? What it is about our time and place that has propelled Coldplay, among many others, to rethink mind-body dualism? Do these speculations on science bear any relation to lead singer Chris Martin and his buddies' fascination with the apocalyptical Johnny Cash? Life is stranger than fiction. Chris and his wife Gwyneth Paltrow named their first child Apple and their second Moses. Eat the fruit and get to the Promised Land—is that the idea?

In this thinking about the decay of the old gods and the emergence of new ones, Christianity has come under scrutiny. Why the fascination with the cross among artists who loathe the God who kills his son (or the man-god who kills himself)? Why do these same artists call for self-erasure and self-forgetting through art as a means to overcome our prosaic present, as a means of achieving an ecstatic, orgiastic, reckless nothingness? What stirs in the soul of a young man and woman when drawn to the cultural artifacts created by these singers, novelists, filmmakers? To put it another way, why does Dave Matthews offer us an album titled *Some Devil*, Tori Amos *Original Sinsuality*, Sarah MacLachlan and Evanescence *Fallen*, James Blunt *Return to Bedlam*, Van Morrison *Pay the Devil*, or Bruce Springsteen *Devils and Dust*—to name but a few? What is NAS up to by appropriating the suffering Christ in *God's Son* and *Street Disciple*. What's up with Busta Rhymes's apocalyptic *Extinction Level Event* and DMX's *It's Dark and Hell is Hot*? This is not even to mention—if we tread back into the mists of pop-culture time—such acts as Black Sabbath, Metallica, Marilyn Manson, Iron Maiden, Judas Priest, Possessed, Napalm Death, and a host of other artists who liked, for example, to suck the blood of chickens on stage while promoting the virtues of necrophilia.

Turn the tube back on. A strange new world of good and evil is emerging that calls into question the very distinction between good and evil. HBO deserves special mention here. *The Sopranos* depicts a world of austerity and lavishness, law and lawlessness, good and evil, that is obfuscated and conflated. In *Carnivale,* a nomadic constellation of misfits travels aimlessly through an America in which occult forces and odd configurations of the natural are a matter of course, and in which they eventually confront a Russian immigrant turned minister, turned Antichrist. *Deadwood* presents us with shady characters searching for gold in a world bereft of government, law, and religion. Then there is the polygamist *Big Love.* One simply waits for the obverse, a show about one wife and several husbands. Think of the possibilities!

This is the world of fantasy, you might say. It does not bear on "reality." But are we not in the midst of a quarrel about the nature of reality itself? Why do so many of us watch—and fantasize about participating in—"reality shows" that expose us to extremes and often appeal to the worst in us, celebrating what we once called vice and exposing the naïveté and inefficacy of virtue? What do we find so attractive about the painful-pleasure aroused when a conniving malcontent is voted off the island (*Survivor*) or out of the house (*Big Brother*)? Or when a partner's propensity to infidelity is exposed on *Temptation Island*? Why do we huddle before the television set to contemplate spectacular feats of transformation when, say, the "reality" of a treadmill is staring us in the face? If you're a tad overweight, snuggle up with a bag of chips and watch *The Big Loser.* If the whole body needs an overhaul, then try *Extreme Makeover.* If only a little grooming is needed, then *Queer Eye for the Straight Guy* is for you—hard to pass up a show about gay men teaching men to be men. Need some wheels for the new look? Try *Pimp My*

Ride or *American Chopper.* Perhaps you are also in need of a new soulmate to go along with the new props? Try *The Bachelor* or *The Bachelorette.* A high-flying job to go with the new accoutrements is surely necessary to complete the fantasy, so just imagine yourself on *The Apprentice.* Or if you're on the way out of the old job, imagine what you might do to *My Big Obnoxious Boss.* If corporate America is not your style, then maybe *American Idol* is your road to stardom; that you also get to vote via text message makes the fantasy all the more intimate and special. If religion is needed to go along with fame, then a few episodes of *Laguna Beach: The* Real *Orange County* should suffice. If the suburbs are obnoxiously bourgeois, then *The 1900 House* or *The Manor House* might do the trick. Or just cut to the chase: live the celebrity life itself with *The Osbornes, The Ashlee Simpson Show, Britney and Kevin,* or Paris Hilton and Nicole Ritchie in *The Simple Life.* "All the world's a stage / And all the men and women merely players."

No, do not make the mistake of thinking about all this as mere entertainment. These shows speak to, and capitalize on, our culture's questions and contradictions about the nature of reality. We believe that gender is a social construction at the same time that we want to assert the distinction between and the uniqueness of the male and the female. We want desperately to see ourselves as the product of our own wills at the same time that we want to see ourselves as natural beings beyond the distorting and alienating effects of civilization. This conflict is captured succinctly in our current fascination with "a return to nature," pursued by means that thwart the very communion we so desperately seek. Stop for a moment to appreciate the irony of a young student so riddled by contradictions that he drives an X-Terra, wears North Face gear, sports Timberland shoes, eats organic, and hikes up a mountain with GPS in hand. Ours is an age that identifies with the artistry of a Jackson Pollock, who threw paint onto a canvas to remind us of the distance between ourselves and what we create. No recognizable form or shape is visible in the work of a Pollock, only an array of colors that speak to the chaos within and beyond.

We could say that all of this amounts merely to a skillful exploitation of those millenarian sensibilities which are always aroused by the passing of a century. Or perhaps America just happens to be the land of both science and enthusiastic religion, and its popular culture simply taps into those assumptions and prejudices for profit. All of this fuss about the end times is therefore of no import and no interest.

I don't think so; in this book, I will argue that there is more at work here than a conventional exploitation of our fears and hopes. The ever-expanding depictions of, ruminations about, and preoccupations with apocalyptic themes we find throughout today's popular culture are, I believe, consequences of our commitment to and dependence upon Enlightenment theology and science. They are not the fruit of a *battle* between the secular and the religious, as we are often told, but a consequence of the curious *affinity* between our secularism and our religiosity. America's dissolution is characterized by a conflation that exposes the shared roots of Enlightenment science and religion. Both are human responses to the Void. Permit me to explain.

the american enlightenment

Conceived within a contentious marriage between Protestant Christianity and the Newtonian Enlightenment, America has evolved into a creature that now looks almost entirely different from its parents. In due course every child steps outside the bounds of parental jurisdiction. Freedom and equality demand no less. In doing so, America has turned against its parents as if enacting a fated role in a Greek tragedy. America inherits and thus depends upon a genetic code, features, and dispositions it now loathes and sees as distinct from itself. The nurturing hand that gives sustenance now looks increasingly like an oppressor. Children return to devour their parents. Such is the nature of our apocalypse.

At first, nothing could seem further from the truth. Chiefly in its Protestant, evangelical, and enthusiastic forms, Christianity has swept across the American landscape so that it now has numerous adherents at the center of our shared political and social lives. And science permeates every aspect of our daily lives; it is embraced by all of us, whether or not we wittingly choose to do so. One might therefore say that the battle between religion and science spells our doom. The problem is in the marriage, not in its constituent parts.

Yet science and religion as they predominate in America are, in fact, bedfellows. American Protestantism has emerged out of the belief that God transcends the bounds of human reason and morality. It is a theological rejection of the baptism of Greek philosophy by biblical revelation, the presiding authorities in that sacramental act being St. Augustine and St. Thomas Aquinas. Beginning with William of Ockham (who

developed a doctrine called Nominalism), and coming to fruition in the writings of John Calvin and Martin Luther, salvation came to be regarded in the Protestant mind as an act of
the will undertaken in the face of an inscrutable universe that
is itself beyond good and evil. We cannot circumscribe an omnipotent God within the bounds of nature. Given the inefficacy
of reason and the dubiousness of passion, we rely on will—a
commitment, a leap of faith, a belief in some revelatory experience that allows us to reach for the divine—for our salvation.
A clash of wills, individual and collective, not of civilizations,
defines our milieu.

Ockham's scientific counterpart is Renè Descartes, best
known for his assertion "Cogito ergo sum," or "I think therefore I am" (in his *Discourse on the Method of Rightly Conducting
One's Reason in the Search for Truth in the Sciences*). Concluding
that the universe cannot be known through common sense and
experience, Descartes nonetheless affirms that he is a thinking being, simply as an act of will. Will is therefore *prior* to
thinking—although his dictum suggests the obverse. Descartes
guides our thoughts by a method—the scientific method. In so
doing, he follows the lead provided by Nominalism, in which
truth is a determination of mind. We cannot have indubitable
knowledge of things in themselves. Mind imposes form on
matter. Descartes' mind/soul and body dichotomy teaches us
to divide human experience into facts (bodies in motion) and
values (the things of the soul), or physics (matter) and metaphysics (spirit). The first part of each dichotomy is concerned
with knowledge, the second is not. Our current fascination with
a return to nature—the pressing desire to embrace something
genuine as a refuge from an artificial world, or the craving for

authenticity, understood as that which stands opposed to the
alienating forces of civilization—grows out of this disjunction
between the self and nature posited by both Enlightenment theology and Enlightenment science.

The search for an Archimedean point in a universe of chaos
and flux—whether this search is to be achieved via a simple
commitment of the will or via reason—breeds dogma. It works
this way: Enlightened Protestantism severs the connection between reason and the soul. If reason and deliberation no longer
serve the spirit, then only the irrational or a-rational can. Unwittingly, Protestantism in this way allies itself with the psy-
chotherapeutic unconscious, and even the occult. In the face of
nothing, the individual flatly affirms belief. We do not connect
with God by works, and certainly not by reason. Rather, we do
so by the moment in time when we *will* such a connection, an
experience that transforms our nature and brings us into communion with divine eternity. In this way, the Enlightenment
breeds a cult of "experiences." Belief in the sovereignty of the
revelatory moment undermines forms, rituals, history, and tradition. Jesus becomes entirely personal.

This is why Americans increasingly refer to themselves as
"spiritual," as opposed to "religious." For in the doctrine of
Enlightened Protestantism, the individual becomes the locus
of transcendent experience. Indeed, the willful individual assumes a sovereignty that makes the context of his actions,
including time, place, and circumstances, increasingly unim-
portant, and finally a hindrance that must be overcome in the
service of a freedom of infinite possibilities. Evangelical and
enthusiastic religions of the "self" become the norm. The Enlightenment is, in fact, the very source of religious fundamen-

talism. The age of reason is by its very nature also the age of unreason.

Science too emerges at, and as, its own Archimedean point. The thinking self is the bright new light that eradicates the darkness of superstition, religiosity, and fanaticism. Instead of random Providence or unruly Fortune, as in premodern times, human society in the age of Enlightenment is governed by what the authors of the Declaration of Independence call the "Laws of Nature and Nature's God." By various instruments and innovations, we capture and utilize the "forces" and "powers" that animate nature. We are Prometheans without punishment and without gods—self-anointed lords and masters of nature. Mathematics assumes its rightful place as the source of intelligibility by providing a language that is not subject to the vagaries of common speech and opinion. Statistics, polls, surveys, and probabilities become the reigning authorities. All other claims to knowledge are brushed off as myths, fantasies, mystifications—in a word, as subjective. Yet this ridicule of the transcendent fuels eruptions of the soul that make little room for reason. Reason demands more than reason can bear.

In fact, the dogmatic character of Enlightenment religion and science precipitates a metamorphosis that calls into question the authority of religion and science. If the divine is a matter of personal experience (or taste, as we now say) then by what means does one adjudicate between respective tastes or experiences? The Bible? Who judges the truth of the Word if the truth is a matter of a personal interpretation, consisting in a personal communion with Jesus that is sovereign over competing doctrinal claims? How do we judge good and evil if an omnipotent God can put evil in the service of good and good in the service of evil? When experience qua experience reigns, it is hardly possible to discriminate between experiences. Therefore, aesthetics replaces morals. Poesis asserts its sovereignty over logos. And the postmodern mind turns this distinction into a disjunction. This book respects the distinction, but questions the disjunction. We must once again begin with the poets.

Protestantism dissolves Protestantism. Science dissolves science. I do not deny the palpable benefits of science. When I am ill I seek a doctor, not a literary critic. The issue here is how science is understood and how that understanding affects our self-understanding as beings with longings, anxieties, joys, sorrows, and hopes. At the beginning of the twentieth century, relativity and quantum physics restored human perspective (contra the mechanistic deism that fascinated early-modern thinkers, such as Galileo and Newton) to its place at the center of all knowing. But this new understanding was achieved at the price of banishing the Absolute. We simultaneously claim to know that we don't know and to know what we know. Science has become at once hegemonic and parochial, universal and particular.

When we penetrate matter itself, we proceed by uncertainty and complementarity expressed in probabilities. Matter dissolves into energy. We speak of "powers" and "forces." Our technological prowess allows us to harness and release the creative and destructive powers that reside in the dark heart of nature. Indeed, we have become both creators and destroyers, authors of holocausts, holding the fates of entire peoples and the planet in our hands. Today the Enlightenment looks less and less enlightened—we are fascinated with chaos, dark matter, black holes, space. The great Void now grips our imagination, without Descartes' illusory security of the willful self. We seek

light in the darkness, hope in the abyss, trying to recreate something out of nothing. But wait—it is God who creates ex nihilo.
Are we ready and able to claim divinity as our own creation?
To create a new scientific metaphysics? A new metaphysical
science? Are we ready for new gods? Are they possible?

form and substance

In this book, I have chosen to tell the story of America's dissolution through artifacts of popular culture, each of which is emblematic of a feature of our Enlightenment—or, if you prefer,
post-Enlightenment—struggle. There are numerous reasons for
taking this route. One is that I wish to speak to students. Another is that popular culture concerns and affects us all—and
perhaps especially those who are not equipped with the aca-
demic body armor that shelters professors from common sense.
In addition, I have chosen not to burden this book with the ap-
paratus of theological and philosophical scholarly jargon and
citations characteristic of books emanating from within the
academy. A concluding bibliographic essay exposes my debts.

My aim, in short, is to help us understand what our iPods
are piping into our veins. We are what we ingest. I am not persuaded by those who peddle the idea that art has no meaning
save what the observer brings to it. Morals and aesthetics are in-
trinsically connected. This connection poses a danger, namely,
the transformation of art into philosophy. But to say that art is
not philosophy does not mean it is not philosophical. In this
book, I try to allow the artists to speak for themselves, and in so
doing to provide access to the logic of their work without depriving their art of its meaning as art. I am interested in stories,

how they work, how they reveal and conceal, how they make us participants by requiring us to think a thought, as opposed to passive readers of a philosopher's statement of a thought. Poets really are, as Percy Shelley claimed, the unacknowledged legislators of the world.

A Consumer's Guide to the Apocalypse is divided into two parts, science and theology. I begin with science and the idea of a soul. Tom Wolfe's *I Am Charlotte Simmons* is a tale of a young woman from Sparta, North Carolina, who enrolls at one of America's elite universities, the fictitious Dupont. Charlotte loses herself as she is absorbed by a reckless and unforgiving social life. Within this larger narrative, Wolfe provides a truncated and provisional history of the science of the self as it has evolved from Darwin to contemporary neuroscience, which seems to leave no room for a self or soul at all. In providing this history, Wolfe juxtaposes Charlotte's fading self with classroom lessons about the self. Intellectually and morally Charlotte is pushed toward the abyss. At one moment, Charlotte even sees herself as nothing. Is this the logical result of a four-year college education today?

I next turn to Michael Frayn's award-winning play *Copenhagen,* a fictitious reconstruction of a controversial and mysterious conversation that did in fact take place between atomic physicists Werner Heisenberg and Niels Bohr in Copenhagen in 1941. Both men are responsible for what has come to be called the Copenhagen interpretation of quantum mechanics, which has two central principles: uncertainty and complementarity. Quantum mechanics has made possible the development of nuclear weapons. But Frayn's main task is not to revisit debates about the creation and use of the atomic bomb. Rather, his play juxtaposes uncertainty and complementarity in physics with uncertainty and complementarity in human relations. We do not know ourselves fully; our motives are often concealed from us, as are those of others. We make use of another's perspective to better comprehend ourselves—we see and judge ourselves and others as beings being seen. Frayn puts into Heisenberg's mouth a question about the possibility of a "quantum ethics." At the limits of reason, Frayn's work implies, we discover that morality is theatrical and sentimental. Nor does Frayn ignore metaphysics. "Uncertainty" leaves room for a negative theology. A dark and cryptic God emerges. We hear the ghost of Hamlet.

We next move from materialistic reductionism to a view of science that points toward a cosmic and mysterious darkness. It is here that the British pop-rockers Coldplay take up the story. Coldplay's music is animated by mystery and set against a cosmic backdrop whose nature eludes the human mind. With Coldplay, we are lost in the cosmos. Coldplay even asks whether we are lost to ourselves. The heart may provide a compass and a destination—love. But for Coldplay, the mind will not leave the heart alone. We discover a tension between the demands of reason and science and the demands of love. For Coldplay, a resolution of these demands proves elusive. We stand before an abyss knowing and not knowing, vacillating between competing demands of our nature, in a universe of beauty and horror, creation and destruction. Are we awaiting new gods?

By the end of Part One, then, we shall have come full circle: from a dying soul to the possibility that science itself may unwittingly rehabilitate the creature it set out to destroy. The first part of the book points to metaphysics, but it does not get us there. This is the task of Part Two, which begins with Dave Matthews and his band. Matthews's songs are lyrical meditations on the contradictory self he thinks we inherit from Christianity. The crucifixion is for Matthews emblematic of our psychological terror, which consists in a curious affinity between love and hate, pain and pleasure, life and death, and among will, resignation, and transcendence. Confusion and despair animate a quest that is simultaneously anti-Christian yet framed within Christian terms. Matthews's music is at odds with itself insofar as he wants to indict and execute the Father while making sense of the erotic violence represented by the cross. This journey takes Matthews to the demonic: behold his first and only solo album, *Some Devil.*

For Matthews, co-opting the Devil is the only means with which to respond to a God who, in the final analysis, is demonic. The distinction between good and evil collapses. Suffering, war, disease, famine provide evidence for the indictment. But how is one good by embodying evil? In the midst of this quandary Matthews searches for silence. He looks for love. He looks for nurture (there are intimations of a lost mother). And of course, he looks for plenty of sex along the way. He ends up courting suicide as the ultimate willful act of simultaneous affirmation and negation, the only act he can appropriate for himself in a meaningless and cruel universe. Matthews, in other words, peddles pious nihilism. He depicts for students the nothingness to which they are naturally drawn by the constricted intellectual and moral horizon of our present.

The same yearning for silence and transcendence informs Chuck Palahniuk's *Fight Club.* His story is of a nameless character, numb as a consequence of his pursuit of perfection. In Palahniuk's effeminized commercial society, the image of perfection is precisely as the market delivers it—cosmetic and ephemeral. But a soul stirs. Unable to find the proper medications to alleviate the pain of his soul, our nameless protagonist visits "Men Remaining Men," a support group for those recovering from testicular cancer. They meet in the basement of the Trinity church. No-name also seeks relief in the basement of the Eucharist church among women with cancer. The choice of locations and genders is not accidental. Our nameless character eventually meets Tyler Durden, a character who exudes an attractive and self-destructive virility. Together, Tyler and no-name start a fight club in bar basements where they can release their anger and self-loathing. As we will see, this elaborate scheme of plots and subplots turns out to be Palahniuk's way of indicting God the Father and the legacy of the crucifixion. His indictment is different from Matthews's insofar as it requires an elucidation of the nature of God as a combination of perverse masculinity and femininity. Indeed, we are moving toward a feminine conclusion. Marla, the last character in the triumvirate, plays a role akin to Eve's in the Garden of Eden. Palahniuk marries a story of self-destruction with a narrative of creation.

Our story concludes with Tori Amos. Taking her bearings from the Gnostic Gospels, and working well before Dan Brown published *The Da Vinci Code,* Amos attempts to recover the forgotten prostitute Mary Magdalene in her battle against a patriarchal Christianity. She does not shun the Virgin Mary but unites her with the Magdalene to create a new image of the feminine that marries the sacred and the profane. Amos seeks to retain her spirituality (the Virgin) along with her sexuality (the Magdalene). The union of Marys makes possible the re-union of body and soul, she implies, a division she believes was imposed by Christianity. Amos rejects the Christian incarnation in favor of a new incarnation. But Amos requires powers to subdue the Christian Father. With the help of a shaman, Amos finds the Dark Prince with whom she joins forces in a psychosexual experience. Her version of the apocalypse is characterized by a fascination with the feminine who possesses a demonic virility with which she slays the tyrant God. As with *Fight Club,* her discography concludes with a reinterpretation of Genesis along Gnostic lines. She recovers Sophia understood not as the cause of the human fall but as a heroine who emancipates us from Christianity's patriarchal tyranny.

Numerous other pop-culture artifacts could be examined in this way, but there is no question that each of these artists' works is well within the pop-culture mainstream. As such, together they shed light on how American culture has been decisively shaped by the legacy of Enlightenment theology and science.

In depicting a curious amalgamation of cosmic and human, physical and metaphysical, religious and scientific phenomena, I hope to expose the Nothing that lies at the origin of the Enlightenment, and to show the curious manner in which science and theology meet after a long history which explains them as fundamentally distinct.

In the end, I hope also to have illustrated and revealed the reasons for some of the central preoccupations about self and society in contemporary America. There is first and foremost a battle for eros. Emancipated sexuality and the obfuscation of gender differences is a function of the Enlightenment's challenge to logos. Fascination with darkness, chaos, quantum physics, black holes, and dark matter in science; with the occult, orgiastic song and dance, gothic iconography, and body piercing in the realm of "spirituality"; and with deconstruction and the resurgence of the poetic over and above the rational in the humanities are manifestations of the essential darkness that the Enlightenment can no longer conceal. A kind of hyperrationality (especially in the social sciences) has taken the place of the judgment, deliberation, and ambiguity that is intrinsic to the very nature of justice. That hyperrationality makes flight to the poetic appealing and compelling. The middle ground is lost: logos is reduced to logic, and poesis to subjective and sentimental affirmations of the self.

In the pages that follow, my endeavor is to restore what has been torn asunder in order to arrive at a premodern or Platonic conclusion, in which poesis is not seen as the antithesis of techne, and logos is severed neither from poesis nor mythos. In other words, poetry is technique inspired by something that is *not* technique. The inspiration for the things we make (in its root, "poetry" literally means "to make") comes from a curious admixture of reason, intuition, and the myths that embody human activity. And for the same reason, the things we make tell us more about ourselves than we often realize.

Part One

Science

News of the Soul's Death
Greatly Exaggerated

America is therefore the one country in the
world where the precepts of Descartes are
least studied and best followed. That should
not be surprising. . . . Americans do not read
Descartes' works because their social state
turns them away from speculative practices,
and they follow his maxims because this same
social state disposes their minds to adopt them.
— Alexis de Tocqueville

om Wolfe is a seer with powers to make his prophe-
cies come true. Such is the nature of the literary mind.
In 1996, *Forbes* magazine published an essay of Wolfe's
titled "Sorry, but Your Soul Just Died" (later collected in
Wolfe's book *Hooking Up*). If we are fascinated by the digital
web that links us all in cyberspace, says Wolfe, just wait. By
"2010, the entire digital universe is going to seem like pretty

mundane stuff compared to a new technology that right now is but a mere glow radiating from a tiny number of American and Cuban (yes, Cuban) hospitals and laboratories" (*Hooking Up,* 89–90). The revolutionary technology is "called brain imaging, and anyone who cares to get up early and catch a truly blinding twenty-first-century dawn will want to keep an eye on it" (90). The dawn came and went. It is a new day and a new world. We now bask in the noonday sun.

Brain imaging "refers to techniques for watching the human brain as it functions, in real time," Wolfe tells us. Invented for medical diagnoses, of "far greater importance is that it may very well confirm, in ways too precise to be disputed, current neuroscientific theories about 'the mind,' 'the self,' 'the soul,' and 'free will.'" This developing science of the brain and nervous system, says Wolfe, "is on the threshold of a unified theory that will have an impact as powerful as that of Darwinism a hundred years ago" (90). Speaking of a "soul" will soon sound as absurd as speaking of witches and warlocks.

How do we find ourselves in such a situation? Neuroscientists, reports Wolfe, begin "with the second most famous statement in all of modern philosophy, Descartes's 'Cogito ergo sum,' 'I think, therefore I am,' which they regard as the essence of 'dualism,' the old-fashioned notion that the mind is something distinct from its mechanism, the brain and the body." Descartes' statement gives rise to the so-called "ghost in the machine" fallacy, "the quaint belief that there is a ghostly 'self' somewhere inside the brain that interprets and directs its operations." Neuroscientists engaged in "three-dimensional electroencephalography will tell you that there is not even any one place in the brain where consciousness or self-consciousness

(*Cogito ergo sum*) is located." Consciousness and self-consciousness are illusions "created by a medley of neurological systems acting in concert" (97). We can mark the success of this understanding of human beings by noting that in 1970, when the Society for Neuroscience was founded, the organization had a meager membership of 1,100. In 1996, Wolfe estimated membership at over 26,000. The impact is felt on college campuses. After all, Wolfe asks, "Why wrestle with Kant's God, Freedom, and Immortality when it is only a matter of time before neuroscience, probably through brain imaging, reveals the actual physical mechanism that fabricates these mental constructs, these illusions?" (98). Philosophy is revealed as pathology—as is religion.

The neuroscientific view emerges in concert with (and may even draw sustenance from) the "most famous statement in all of modern philosophy: Nietzsche's 'God is dead.'" According to Wolfe, Nietzsche's claim is not a statement of atheism, though an atheist he was. Rather, Nietzsche simply brings "news of an event." The news was that "educated people no longer believed in God, as a result of the rise of rationalism and scientific thought, including Darwinism, over the preceding 250 years" (98). Nietzsche is by no means sanguine about this fact. In his autobiographical *Ecce Homo* he predicts, Wolfe notes, "that the twentieth century would be a century of 'wars such as have never happened on earth,' wars catastrophic beyond all imagining." Unable to surrender our guilt to God, we turn our revenge on one another. The age of total war coincides with the "'total eclipse of all values.'" If we doubt Nietzsche's predictive powers, Wolfe invites us to consider the "world wars of the twentieth century and the barbaric brotherhoods of

Nazism and Communism. Ecce vates! *Ecce vates!* Behold the prophet! How much more proof can one demand of a man's powers of prediction?" (99).

In telling the story of the ascent of neuroscience, the demise of Freudianism and Marxism—and with them, the entire belief in social conditioning—is of principal concern to Wolfe (100–103). Rather than explain the maladies of the "self" by reference to a social environment, neuroscience redirects our attention back to the body. To be sure, this shift in emphasis does not deny the importance of environment in shaping our biological endowment, an issue we will return to shortly. But a renewed emphasis on the body does have implications for our capacity for self-government. The issues raised by neuroscience are not simply epistemological or biological. They are political. Wolfe writes:

> The notion of a self—a self who exercises self-discipline, postpones gratification, curbs the sexual appetite, stops short of aggression and criminal behavior—a self who can become more intelligent and lift itself to the very peaks of life by its own bootstraps through study, practice, perseverance, and refusal to give up in the face of great odds—this old-fashioned notion (what's a *boot*strap for God's sake?) of success through enterprise and true grit is already slipping away, slipping away . . . slipping away. . . . The peculiarly American faith in the power of the individual to transform himself from a helpless cipher into a giant among men, a faith that ran from Emerson ("Self-Reliance") to Horatio Alger's *Luck and Pluck* stories to Dale Carnegie's *How to Win Friends and Influence People* to Norman Vincent Peale's *The Power of Positive Thinking* to Og Mandino's *The Greatest Salesman in the World*—that faith is now as moribund as the god for whom Nietzsche wrote an obituary in 1882. (104)

By this circuitous route we come to Wolfe's own prophecy:

> [I]n the year 2010 or 2030, some new Nietzsche will step for-
> ward to announce: "The self is dead"—except that being prone
> to the poetic, like Nietzsche the First, he will probably say: "The
> soul is dead." He will say that he is merely bringing the news,
> the news of the greatest event of the millennium: "The soul,
> that last refuge of values, is dead, because educated people no
> longer believe it exists." (107)

the quarrel between philosophy and poetry

That new poetic Nietzsche just might be Wolfe himself. Rough-
ly ten years removed from the *Forbes* essay, Wolfe delivered
a bold and daring book, *I Am Charlotte Simmons,* that depicts
the consequences of the death of the soul and God. Wolfe's
book tells the story of a young teenage high school graduate
from Sparta, North Carolina. The novel chronicles Charlotte
Simmons's journey from a small Southern town where the old
virtues of religion, patriotism, austerity, and self-command
reign to one of America's elite universities, a place that, like
most elite universities in America, is steeped in "political cor-
rectness." The emphasis that Wolfe placed, in his *Forbes* essay,
on what "educated persons" believe points to why the modern
university is the novel's proper setting. This is the arena where
intellectual movements take root and are spread among rising
generations. It is also the place where the young put their newly acquired lessons into practice. Charlotte may have arrived
at Dupont University with a soul. But after less than a year,
the stifling social and intellectual atmosphere asphyxiates that

original breath of life which is the source of moral integrity and emancipates her latent lawlessness. Her nascent moral and intellectual longings crushed, Charlotte emerges at the end of the novel animated by little more than a Nietzschean "will to power," courting recognition for its own sake, appearance substituting for moral substance.

At first glance, *I Am Charlotte Simmons* seems to be a translation of Wolfe's *Forbes* essay into novel form. Wolfe himself provides evidence for this interpretation. Within the first hundred pages (what counts for an introduction in Wolfe's terms), we learn that Charlotte is enrolled in a course taught by Dr. Lewin titled "Modern French Novel: From Flaubert to Houellebecq." For the day's discussion, Lewin has assigned Flaubert's *Madame Bovary*, a work that is arguably among the first modern novels and depicts a nascent modernity that ends in suicide. That Wolfe has Lewin select Flaubert—and Houellebecq—is no accident. Let us listen in:

> "For a moment [Lewin begins] let's consider the very first pages of *Madame Bovary*. We're in a school for boys . . . The very first sentence says"—he pushed the glasses back up on his forehead and brought the book back up under his chin, close to his myopic eyes—"'We were at preparation, when the headmaster came in, followed by a new boy dressed in "civvies" and a school servant carrying a big desk.' And so forth and so on . . . uhmmm, uhmmm"—he kept his face down in the book—"and then it says, 'In the corner behind the door, only just visible, stood a country lad of about fifteen, taller than any of us—.'"

Lewin notes that Flaubert begins the book with "We were at preparation," and "taller than us," referring to Charles Bovary's schoolmates. But then, Lewin continues, Flaubert "never tells the story in the first person plural again, and after a few pages we never see any of these boys again. Now, can anybody tell me why Flaubert uses this device?" (99). Charlotte answers:

> Well, I think he does it that way because what the first chapter really is, is Charles Bovary's background up to the time he meets Emma, which is when the real story begins. The last two-thirds of the chapter are written like a plain-long biography, but Flaubert didn't want to start the book that way . . . because he believed you should get your point across by writing a real vivid scene with just the right details. The point of the first chapter is to show that Charles is a country bumpkin and always has been and always will be, even though he becomes a doctor and everything. . . . "*Une de ces pauvres choses, enfin, dont la laideur muette a des profondeurs d'expression . . . comme le visage d'un imbécile.*" So you start the book seeing Charles the way we—the other boys—saw him, and the way *we* saw him is so vivid that all the way through the book, you never forget that what Charles is, is a hopeless fool, an idiot. (100–101)

Lewin is aghast. Wolfe makes it clear that these are not the kinds of intelligent responses professors at elite universities expect. "Thank you. . . . That's *precisely* why. Flaubert never simply *explained* a key point if he could *show* it instead, and to show it he needed a *point of view*" (101).

It would seem that Wolfe's novel is a demonstration of the lessons of "Sorry, but Your Soul Just Died." But appearances are deceiving.

Upon its publication, conservatives lauded *I Am Charlotte Simmons* as a fitting testimony to the failure of American higher education to provide a moral setting for young teenagers. Liberals vilified Wolfe for the puerile imagination it allegedly revealed (Wolfe is not shy about revealing the absence of shame that is the fruit of our wallowing in the body); after all, Wolfe is now in his seventies, and by virtue of his age alone cannot possibly understand the mind and mores of the rising generation. But these partisan attempts to eulogize or vilify Wolfe ignored several key features of the novel that give it a subtle and not readily perceptible complexity. When considering the "self" as envisioned and propagated by neuroscientists, Wolfe raises some vexed questions that call into question the soundness of scientific reductionism and materialism. In this respect, *I Am Charlotte Simmons* goes well beyond the *Forbes* essay in showing the perils of reducing humans to animals. Wolfe does not now deny the explanatory power of scientific reductionism. But he does expose the dangers that arise when humans no longer believe themselves to be spiritual creatures.

Wolfe's response to materialism and reductionism, then, is neither to adopt a disembodied idealism nor to take pietistic refuge in religion. Rather, there is evidence to suggest that Wolfe is concerned with the Protestant assault on the medieval or Catholic synthesis of faith and reason. By placing religious sensibilities out of the reach of reason, Protestant theology makes a curious and unwitting alliance with modern antirationalism. Yet Wolfe does not arrive at a Catholic or medieval conclusion. Given the fact that, under Protestantism, Christianity has become a religion of the willful self, Wolfe takes another route toward the rediscovery of the soul. In fact, his book is curiously Socratic, infused with faint but audible suggestions about the importance of the classical Greek heritage in higher education, understood as distinct from the effort by Christians to baptize Greek philosophy. In this book, at least, as opposed to his previous novel, *A Man in Full,* Wolfe is less Stoic than he is Greek.

i am therefore i think

Let us return to the beginning. The title of Wolfe's novel is, in my estimation, a reference to Descartes' "I think, therefore I am." Descartes' dictum is, for philosophers and scientists alike, the fountainhead of mind-body dualism (or perhaps we should say dichotomy). The separation between body and mind is now typically regarded as one of the most pernicious and misleading developments in Western philosophy. We are more enlightened these days; we speak of "Descartes' Error" and of the "embodied mind." The title of the novel indicates that Descartes is also the starting point for Wolfe's own meditation on mind-body duality. Throughout the novel we find various protagonists struggling to contend with the contradictory pulls of their passions and their reason. Indeed, Aristotle, often cited as an authority on the relationship between moral and intellectual virtue, makes a crucial appearance that brings the struggle between the rational and arational faculties forcefully into view (589–90). Wolfe, in other words, wishes to reflect on our Cartesian heritage in an effort to discern the connection between mind and body.

Unlike our neuroscientific brethren, however, Wolfe is no reductionist. A trinity of mind, body, and culture immediately supplants dualism in this work. In the "Foreword," Wolfe introduces us to Victor Ransome Starling, who we later learn is Charlotte's professor in the course "Descartes, Darwin, and the

Mind-Body Problem." Wolfe's "Foreword" is supposedly taken from *The Dictionary of Nobel Laureates* (a publication that actually exists but does not include this fictitious entry). Back in 1983, we are told, Professor Starling "surgically removed the amygdala, an almond-shaped mass of gray matter deep within the brain that controls emotions in the higher mammals, from thirty cats" (3). When our mammalian brethren are surgically altered in this way, they "veer helplessly from one inappropriate affect to another." Extracting the amygdala induces "boredom where there should be fear, cringing where there should be preening, sexual arousal where there was nothing that would stimulate an intact animal" (3). The amygdalectomized cats, we are told, enter into a state of "sexual arousal hypermanic in the extreme." The surgically altered cats attempt copulation with "such frenzy, a cat mounted on another cat would be in turn mounted by a third cat, and that one by yet another, and so on, creating tandems (colloq., 'daisy chains') as long as ten feet." When the men in white coats released thirty normal cats "used as controls," Starling's assistant soon discovered that the normal cats mimicked the behavior of the amygdalectomized cats. "In that moment originated," we read in the fictitious entry, "a discovery that has since radically altered the understanding of animal and human behavior: the existence—indeed, pervasiveness—of 'cultural para-stimuli'" (4). Starling's experiment shows that "a strong social or 'cultural' atmosphere, even as abnormal as this one, could in time overwhelm the *genetically determined* responses of perfectly normal, healthy animals" (4, emphasis added). Fourteen years later Professor Starling had become the "twentieth member of the Dupont faculty awarded the Nobel Prize" (4).

With this discussion of Starling's work, Wolfe zeros in on a part of the brain that decodes emotional stimuli, chiefly fear and pleasure. The amygdala may be Wolfe's stand-in for Descartes' pineal gland, the organ in the brain where Descartes believed body and soul met. But we are not done with Professor Starling. In our next encounter with him, Wolfe raises another important question about the relationships among culture, mind, body, and brain. Who or what distinguishes and adjudicates between the competing parts of the "self"? Wolfe depicts the principal protagonist reading from a text for her course on "Descartes, Darwin, and the Mind-Body Problem." Eating an earthy breakfast of "health-nut bread, which seemed to be made of dried husks" (Wolfe's novel is replete with these wonderful juxtapositions), Charlotte comes to the following passage:

> Whereas the doctrine that cultural changes represent nothing more than the organism's constant probing in the process of natural selection begs the question of whether or not the "mind" is in any way autonomous, the argument that "minds" are capable, through a process of organized "wills," of creating cultural changes wholly independent of that process revives, ultimately, the discredited notion of the ghost in the machine. (220)

The conclusion to which Wolfe draws us may be that "the ghost in the machine" has not been exorcised. We are beings of nature and culture, yet we seem to ourselves to be beings beyond nature and culture. Freedom or autonomy is borne of the capacity to transcend nature and culture. What, then, is that "will" which directs the machine to do what it ought to do as opposed to what it merely desires? What prompts us to choose in opposition to the dictates of culture or of nature? For Wolfe—and for us—nothing less than the possibility of human freedom is at stake in the challenge, set forth lucidly in Charlotte's textbook, raised by the scientific conception of the self. Consider how often Charlotte utters the phrase "I am Charlotte Simmons" (cf. 342, 425 for a poignant comparison). We too must ask: who or what am I? The reader might chuckle at the observation that the favorite watering hole of the Dupont student body is called the "I.M.", which may be mistaken for a reference to "Instant Messaging" (271). O Dionysus!

scientific faith

According to Wolfe the essayist, we "now live in an age in which science is a court from which there is no appeal." The existential dilemmas of the human condition are increasingly brought before the tribunal science, and for good reason (96). The magistrates of science are able to alter the brain and thus deal with maladies of the mind once under the sovereignty of various occult practices—psychoanalysis and religion among them. Psychopharmacology, for example, alters the chemistry of the brain and either cures or ameliorates various mental disorders. Is this not ample evidence that mind is reducible to brain? *I Am Charlotte Simmons* responds to the magistrates of the High Court of Science in two ways, neither of which are intended to be decisive or conclusive. Wolfe introduces us to two episodes in the "science of the self" that invite us to think further about the limits of mind-body dualism, the implications of the trinity of mind, body, and culture he has introduced, and the prospects for free will.

In the first episode, we find Professor Starling lecturing on the contributions of José Manuel Rodriguez Delgado, former director of neuropsychiatry at the Yale University Medical School and author of the *Physical Control of the Mind: Toward a Psychocivilized Society* (389). This controversial book (which is real, as is the author) is concerned with the possibility and potential benefits of mind control. If we know what the mind does, and in knowing learn to control what it does, why not fashion human beings so as to eliminate the undesirable and enhance the desirable qualities of their minds? Starling speaks of Delgado as "one of those scientists who faced death—or so it seemed to other people—by using themselves as guinea pigs to test their own discoveries" (390). He is one of rationalism's disciples, one of those men with "such *faith* in the empirical validity of their physical knowledge and their own powers of logic . . . [that] they had no more fear than the conjurer who swallows fire . . ." (390–91, my emphasis). The pursuit of reason, in other words, is guided by faith in reason. We do not begin by knowing but by not knowing. Enter Cartesian doubt. Faith is camouflaged but present in the realm of science, just as it is in the desire for transcendence.

As Charlotte listens to his lecture, Starling projects onto a screen an image of a bullfighting ring with a couple dozen people in the stands. On one side of the ring we find a charging bull, on the other "a man in a white smock standing stock-still and holding a small black object in his hands at waist level" (391). An indignant student yelps, "Oh—my—God!" and then proceeds to pass judgment on the barbarity of the spectacle (391). To which Starling replies: "*That's* your reaction to a culture different from your own?" (391). He then lectures the student on the virtues of tolerance, and by implication on the necessity of an "objective" view of the matter. Here, then, democratic tolerance meets cultural determinism, respect for diversity links up with universal science. That education often mystifies more than it enlightens, Wolfe implies, should not surprise either students or their parents.

The image on the screen is of a photograph taken in 1955. Delgado, Starling explains, "has implanted an electrode in the bull's caudate nucleus, which is just under the amygdala." The bull is "charging full tilt." When the bull "came close enough to make it interesting," Starling continues, "Delgado pressed a button on the little radio transmitter in his hand, and the bull's aggressiveness vanished," Starling snaps his fingers, "like *that*." Another image is put on the screen that shows "[t]he animal's legs . . . bent in the attitude of a lazy canter." Starling notes that the bull's "anger has vanished" (392). Responding to his own query about the meaning of this experiment, he says: "The instantaneous lesson was that an emotion as powerful as a raging urge to kill can be turned off . . . by stimulating a particular area of the brain." More importantly, the experiment demonstrates that "emotions but also *purpose* and *intentions* are *physical* matters" (396). The emphases are Wolfe's. Starling's conclusions, if they are correct, clearly falsify any supernatural conception of mind.

Delgado is said to have been aware of the "philosophical implications" of the experiment (393), which shows that the propensity to think of mind as the command center of the brain is a "useful illusion" (393). In truth, the self is "nothing more than a 'transient composite of materials from the environment.' It's not a command center but a village marketplace, an arcade, or a lobby, like a hotel lobby, and other people and their ideas and their mental atmosphere and the Zeitgeist—the spirit of the age, to use Hegel's term from two hundred years ago—can come walking right on in, and *you* can't lock the doors, because *they* become *you,* because they *are* you" (393). Wolfe is perhaps suggesting that there is more to mind than brain. And he does so by showing us that thoughts are things. This is not necessarily a return to mind-body dualism. The point here is that thoughts are real.

Wolfe's juxtaposition of brain stimulation with the spirit of the age—the Zeitgeist—is odd. I am inclined to think it is deliberate. Wolfe is perhaps suggesting that there is more to mind than brain. And he does so by showing us that thoughts are things—invisible (like a soul), but curiously palpable. Throughout his book we find "persons" going in and out of each other's minds, "persons" absorbing the thoughts of others. Invisible currents of thought seem to be everywhere. Read carefully chapter 16, aptly titled "The Sublime" (320–33), wherein we find two basketball players trying to "psyche each other out," as we say. And consider in this context the word *sublime* as it is used in the sciences. In chemistry, sublimation is the transformation of a solid into a vapor without passing through the liquid stage. In chapter 16, Charlotte is liquid; she sheds tears. That chapter concludes: "The sublime was called Charlotte Simmons" (333).

This peculiar chapter 16 is reminiscent of C. S. Lewis's famous reflection on education, *The Abolition of Man*, in which he argues that we have become persons without chests, becoming either all groin or all brain. Human beings seem to be *more* than body and mind put together. There is a seat of adjudication at the center of the human person which both rationalists and sentimentalists ignore. Call it the heart or call it the soul. Consider how many times Wolfe refers to the solar plexus. That Charlotte goes from one state to another but bypasses the center speaks to what she is losing throughout the book: her soul, her core, the seat of judgment. The use of that all-too-Freudian term *sublimation*—referring to what is "sub" or below—also points to what humans can intuit but cannot see. Freud reduced the soul to sex or libido. Wolfe does not. Keep sublimation in mind as we move through the second part of the book.

By describing an episode in the life of another of Charlotte's friends, in this case the star basketball player Jojo Johansen, Wolfe brings us back to the body, yet without collapsing Word into Flesh or Flesh into Word. Jojo is enrolled in a course at Dupont titled "The Age of Socrates." Himself christened "Socrates" by his coach, Jojo, who has been assigned Aristotle's *Metaphysics,* is ruminating on Professor Margolies' lecture on the nature of "concepts" and "conceptual thinking" (589). "The age of Socrates was the age of the first systematic thought," the narrator informs us. "By the very way they thought, the Greeks changed the world" (589), reflecting mind's imprint on matter. Jojo returns to the *Metaphysics.* "Socrates did not make the universals or the definitions exist apart; Plato, however, gave them separate existence, and this was the kind of thing they called Ideas" (589). Plato (not Socrates) establishes that mind must be prior to experience, we are told.

But as Jojo continues reading his Aristotle, the Platonic claim begins to unravel. "As man's body is composed of materials gathered from the material world, so man's reason is part of the universal Reason or Mind of the world" (590). At that very moment when we think we will emerge from the cave into the full light of the sun, to that region of being where we contemplate the Forms, Wolfe drags us back into the artificial light of the cave. We return to the *Metaphysics.* "Socrates overlooked the irrational parts of the soul . . . and did not take sufficient notice of the fact of the weakness of man, which leads him to do what he knows to be wrong" (590). Jojo then thinks that statement over with some difficulty: "Socrates just got through saying man's reason is what it's all about, not false happiness . . . and all of a sudden here's Aristotle saying moral weakness . . . is what it's all about" (590). Jojo is puzzled. The reader is invited to consider the same puzzle.

Let us do Wolfe justice by leaving that ambiguity just as it is. Consider another question: why is Wolfe's book replete with references to bodily functions? These references, often vulgar, nauseate some readers. But Wolfe's reduction of the various protagonists to animals, ape-like creatures who copulate indiscriminately and incessantly, who perpetually use the "F" word and the "S" word to describe their thoughts and experiences, is his way of deliberately evoking a reaction against the scientific reduction of human beings to their bodies. He realizes that not only will the prudish or chaste be disgusted by that reduction, but the partisans of freedom as well. Freedom cannot consist in enslavement to the urges of the body. What does it mean to think of human beings in terms of such concepts as dignity, nobility, virtue? Wolfe invites questions about the nature of thought, but he does not end up in some idyllic place. He is in the cave. As the previous episodes illustrate, there is a curious middle, a distinctly human middle, elegantly captured by the Aristotelian mean. That place eludes Jojo. But it should not elude us.

before the "is" and before the "i"

Wolfe's engagement with Darwin raises a related but different question about the reduction of humans to their bodies: is there a difference between what "is" and what is "created"? We return yet again to Professor Starling. On this occasion, we find him employing the "Socratic approach," as if he were speaking to "twelve or thirteen souls gathered around a seminar table rather than the 110 who now sat before him in steep tiers." His students fill "a small but grandiose amphitheater with a dome and a ceiling mural by Annigoni of Daedalus and the flight of Icarus from the labyrinth of Minos," writes Wolfe, who in this way allows the ancients to hover over Starling's account of the theory of evolution. According to Starling, "Darwin describes evolution in terms of a 'tree of life,' starting with a single point from which rise limbs, branches . . . offshoots of infinite variety" (280). He then ponders: "What is that *point* where it all starts? What does Darwin say this tree of life has ascended *from*? Where does he say evolution begins?" (280).

A female student responds: "He said it began with a single cell, a single cell organism. . . . Somebody asked him where the single cell was located, and he said, 'Oh, I don't know, probably in a warm pond somewhere'" (280–81). Starling corroborates the student's response, and then goes on to ask: "Where did Darwin say the single cell or cells came from?" (281). Charlotte responds, "Darwin said—he said he didn't know where the original cells came from, and he wasn't going to guess?" (281). According to Charlotte, the question of the origin of life "was a hopeless inquiry?" "And I think he said," Charlotte continues, "in *The Origin of the Species*?—I think he said that in the beginning it was the Creator?—with a capital C? It was the Creator, and he breathed life 'into a few or into one'—a *few* single-cell organisms or *one* single-cell organism, I guess" (282). Starling concurs:

You'll notice that Darwin, who probably did more than any other single person to extinguish religious faith among educated people, doesn't present himself as an atheist. He bows to "the Creator." He always professed to be a religious person. There's one school of thought that says he was only throwing a sop to the conventional beliefs of his day, since he knew *The Origin of the Species* might be attacked as blasphemous. (282)

Whatever the truth of the matter, Starling emphasizes that, even for Darwin, the "origin of the species, which is to say, evolution, and the origin of life itself, of the impulse to live, are two different things" (282). In other words, a reasonable response to the limits of knowledge is skepticism, not dogmatic atheism. Socrates, not Nietzsche.

Dogmatic atheism, however, is the prevailing spirit among neuroscientists, as Wolfe depicts them. He describes, in a provocative passage, the shift from Darwin's own skepticism or agnosticism to the new dogma of our time:

Darwin was not a neuroscientist. His knowledge of the human brain, if any, was primitive. He knew nothing about genes, even though they were discovered by a contemporary of his, an Austrian monk named Gregor Johann Mendel—whose work strengthens the case for evolution tremendously. But Darwin did something more fundamental. He obliterated the cardinal distinction between man and the beasts of the fields and the wilds. It had always been a truism that man is a rational being

and animals live by "instinct." But what is instinct? It's what
we now know to be the genetic code an animal is born with.
In the second half of the last century, neuroscientists began to
pursue the question, "If man is an animal, to what extent does
his genetic code, unbeknownst to him, control his life?" Enormously, according to Edward O. Wilson, a man some speak
of as Darwin the Second. . . . But there is a big difference between "enormously" and "entirely." "Enormously" leaves some
wiggle room for your free will to steer your genetically coded
"instincts" in any direction you want—if there is such a thing
as "you." I say "if," because the new generation of neuroscientists—and I enjoy staying in communication with them—believe
Wilson is a very cautious man. They laugh at the notion of free
will. They yawn at your belief—my belief—that each of us has
a capital-letter I, as in "I believe," a "self," inside our head that
makes "you," makes "me," distinct from every other member of
the species Homo sapiens, no matter how many ways we might
be like them. The new generation are absolutists. (283)

Wolfe concludes these reflections with an anecdote that
sums up the consequences of the abolition of the self as a gen-
uinely free, rational, and autonomous being. Starling receives
an e-mail from one of the new generation of absolutists, which
he shares with the class. "Let's say you pick up a rock and you
throw it. And in mid-flight you give that rock consciousness
and a rational mind. That little rock will think it has free will
and will give you a highly rational account of why it has decided to take the route it's taking." To such scientific absolutists,
in other words, we are but particles in motion with predeter-
mined trajectories, until we clash with other, similar particles.
To describe human behavior accurately is simply to engage in

a complicated kind of physics. *Copenhagen* is next. Starling asks the class to consider, as Wolfe does the reader: "'Am I really . . . merely . . . a conscious little rock?' The answer, Starling continues, 'has implications of incalculable importance for the Homo sapiens' conception of itself and for the history of the twenty-first century'" (283).

method over substance

The authority of science, and neuroscience, is established partly by what scientists say, and partly by the manner in which they say it, i.e., the scientific method. The scientific method is supposedly independent of the prejudices of a scientist since, in principle, it can be duplicated by anyone. Moreover, science presents its findings in mathematical terms, which allows it to overcome the problems caused by variability in the meaning and interpretation of words. There are good reasons why scientists speak confidently of their "objectivity," and why nonscientists often find themselves deferring to or embarrassed by them. It is not simply that the likes of Delgado and Darwin and those who follow them tell a good story. They have a method that provides many advantages over the murky prose of a humanist. But lost in most discussions of the superiority of the scientific method is an understanding of the extent to which science is art and art science.

We take up Wolfe's reflections on this matter by returning to the classroom. The "peripatetic" Starling is discussing the origins of sociobiology, a field of scientific study developed by the aforementioned Edward O. Wilson. As a newly minted Ph.D. teaching at Harvard, Wilson took a research trip to a place in the Caribbean known as "Monkey Island." He went there to "help his first graduate student launch a study of macaque rhesus monkeys in their natural habitat." Wilson had been himself primarily preoccupied with ants, but this journey seems to prompt a move up the Chain of Being. With his assistant, Wilson discussed the "similarities—despite the enormous differences in size, strength, and intelligence—between ants and apes" (619). Starling goes on to describe what came out of those conversations. "Wilson experienced what every research scientist lives for . . . the *Aha!* phenomenon, that flash of synthesis that will revolutionize the field. If there are similarities—analogies—between the social lives of ants and apes, why wouldn't Homo sapiens be part of the same picture? The analogies came flooding to his mind" (619).

But science is not science as long as analysis remains on the level of analogy. Science separates itself from the humanities by virtue of a particular method and by the authority of mathematics. With a mischievous smile, Starling continues:

> But just as Nature abhors a vacuum, Science abhors analogies. Analogies are regarded as superficial, as "literary," which to the scientific mind—and certainly to Wilson's—means impressionistic. Now . . . since Science abhors analogies, just how did Wilson go about showing that from ants to humans the social life of all animals was similar—and more than similar, in fact, since in all animals it was part of a single biological system? (619)

To Charlotte's chagrin, a perky, flirtatious woman with a "Savannah deb-party accent" weighs in with the answer. Wilson banishes analogies by the use of "allometry," which our perky Southerner describes as "the study of the relative growth of a part of an organism in relation to the growth of the whole"

(620). Allometry enabled Wilson to do the "submarine" says the young woman to the amusement of all present. "He went down . . . under the anecdotal level, the surface level? . . . and found mathematically corroborant first principles? . . . and that way he doesn't . . . *have* to say an ant is like a human being or that a . . . . a . . . I don't know . . . a baboon is like a sea slug?—because he can show that behavior at *that* evolutionary level is demonstrably—or I reckon I should say allometrically?—the same as behavior at this evolutionary level . . . seems like to me" (620). Mathematics—allometry—gives science the authority it lacks as a prescientific, mythical, allegorical, literary description of the universe. Wolfe does not question the authority of mathematical science, but he does provoke the reader to reconsider the finality that mathematics purports to provide. We find security in numbers, symbols, and equations. But in the grand scheme of things, is it a false sense of security? In light of our search for truth or logical rigor, it behooves us to remember that scientific theories do not purport to give us the finality often implied by those very theories. As Starling says to the young Charlotte, in science "'no theory merits consideration unless you can provide a set of contradictions, which, if true, would prove it wrong'" (344). We seek to falsify in the service of truth.

the city of god

You have probably been thinking about religion while reading this discussion of Wolfe's attitude toward science. If you are a partisan of science, you may even be alarmed by the implications of Wolfe's discussion; if it is credible, it seems to make science akin, in important ways, to our "irrational" beliefs. This interpretation threatens our understanding and practice of science as science. Wolfe emerges as the enemy of reason. Partisans of the view that science is a human activity, practiced in a human context, and therefore inextricably linked to moral ends, might even see Wolfe as a fellow traveler, if not a comrade in arms.

This appropriation of Wolfe as a moral conservative is understandable. There are scenes in the novel that seem to support the view that the threats to Charlotte Simmons's moral self-understanding might find solutions and alternatives in religion. Ponder, for example, the disturbing and ironic chapter 26, "How Was It?" (491–520). Here, Wolfe has Charlotte reflect on the raucous events of a senior formal, the details of which I will spare the reader. In this chapter, Charlotte contemplates the prospects of being *"damned"* (500). Instead of asserting, "I am Charlotte Simmons," as she has often done before, in this chapter she says *"Ecce* Charlotte Simmons" (502). She stares into the abyss, yearns for the no-thing. She has arrived at nihilism. Coming from what was a wholesome Sparta in which belief in God and country reigned, Charlotte cannot find what kind of person she is in a corrupt Athens. The allusion to *Ecce Homo,* or "Behold the Man," is, I believe, less a reference to Pilate's announcement that here is the Christ crowned with thorns than it is a reference to the title of Nietzsche's autobiographical *Ecce Homo.* Wolfe's essay "Sorry, but Your Soul Just Died" supports this reading by its explicit references to Nietzsche and the "death of God." Wolfe places Charlotte's "damnation" in chapter 26 alongside a conversation between the Jewish president of Dupont, Frederick Culter, the Jewish professor Jerry Quat, and the Waspish basketball coach Buster Roth, which serves to point us toward America's Judeo-Christian heritage. That juxtaposition is not accidental. Nor is the poverty of their discussion.

There are two curious passages in *I Am Charlotte Simmons* that lead me to wonder whether the conservative appropriation of Wolfe is legitimate. These passages bring us back to my concluding remarks in the section "From Prophesy to Incarnation," where I suggest that Wolfe appears to take issue with the Protestant assault on reason. In the first passage, we find Charlotte wandering through the library, haunted by recent events that I'll not detail in order to preserve the book's secrets. Charlotte is not wholly herself. She is poignantly aware that her body is moving but her mind is elsewhere. Absentmindedly, she crashes into her friend Adam. Here is the First Man. The stack of books Adam is carrying falls to the floor. Charlotte apologetically moves to pick them up, simultaneously trying to explain why she is in distress. Adam tells her not to worry about the scattered books and explains:

> Nobody'll touch them. They're all full of arcane religious history. Nobody will know what a matrix is in those books. Henry's break with Rome was the most important event in modern history. All of modern science flows from that. People don't get the point of all the pioneers of human biology being Englishmen and Dutchmen—oh . . . (563)

What does Wolfe want us to learn from the great divide between Protestants and Catholics? We could say that Wolfe endorses the Protestant Reformation because he endorses science. The separation of reason from faith allows each to proceed on separate courses. But the novel as a whole is not friendly to materialistic reductionism. Is there some pre-Reformation insight that Wolfe wants us to grasp? Before the Protestant belief took hold that we could begin to access a personal God through faith alone, theologians of a different stripe put philosophy in the service of faith. Augustine did so via neo-Platonism, and Aquinas did so via Aristotle. Perhaps Wolfe is thinking out new ways in which reason and faith might become reconnected?

The second passage, which also harkens back to a kind of pre-Reformation unity of faith and reason, concerns Charlotte's relationship to a fellow student named Hoyt Thorpe, a thuggish, lecherous, and pretentious frat-boy who aspires to be an investment banker/financial analyst. An economics major, Hoyt is among the elite at Dupont and represents a new class of Americans defined by wealth they did not earn, the fruits of which only magnify their vulgarity and lack of culture. Hoyt, like his fraternity brothers, considers himself a "master of the universe" or a "man in full," to refer to two enduring themes in Wolfe's work. Hoyt is president of the revered Saint Raymond fraternity, named, most likely, after Saint Raymond of Penafort (1175–1275). After a violent encounter with Hoyt, Charlotte takes refuge at Adam's house in the "City of God" (363, 373), a residential area adjacent to the university. It is likely that students at Dupont associate the "City of God" with a film bearing the same title (directed by Fernando Meirelles and Katiá Lund, 2002) about gang warfare in the "favelas" or slums of Rio de Janeiro. They are not likely to think first of Augustine's magisterial work. But at least some of Wolfe's readers will. Is Augustine here because Wolfe wants us to think of his philosophical influence (via the neo-Platonists), Plato? And from there back to Socrates?

Wolfe places Charlotte Simmons in the academy, where the ancient Greek philosophers exist as mere shadows, images with no vitality or power to influence us. The final exorcism of pagan ghosts occurred during the Protestant Reformation, which razed the meeting place for reason and faith. We ought to be grateful. For compelling reasons, not least the barbarity carried out in the name of God, science did not and cannot let irrationalism be. But is religion merely a form of irrationalism? Is that the only alternative to science? Or, rather, might it be possible to re-create a meeting place for open-minded scientists and thoughtful believers? Socrates may be dead, but perhaps we still have reason to hope; after all, students still dream.

Knowledge of Ignorance

Observation and experience can and must
drastically restrict the range of admissible
scientific belief, else there would be no more
science. But they cannot determine a particular body of such belief. An apparently arbitrary
element, compounded by person and historical accident, is always a formative ingredient
of the beliefs espoused by a given scientific
community at a given time
— Thomas Kuhn

I n declaring for themselves a "separate and equal" station
among the powers of the earth, for what reasons do the
authors of the Declaration of Independence appeal to the
"Laws of Nature and of Nature's God"? Arguably, Thomas
Jefferson and the principal draftsmen of that document drew
inspiration from the philosophers of the Enlightenment, especially its principal luminaries Thomas Hobbes and John Locke,
according to whom we may conquer chance by the application

of the laws of nature to human affairs and, consequently, deliver to the world a genuine *science* of politics. The concept of science, for Enlightenment thinkers like Hobbes, Locke, and Jefferson, referred to those revolutionary speculations from Galileo to Newton that had come to govern natural philosophy. The Laws of Nature and of Nature's God, they believed, govern individuals and society in the same way they do the physical universe. Science is thus placed in the service of political mastery.

This is a curious development. For what could individual agency or freedom mean if eternal and immutable laws *determine* our actions? A mechanical universe does not leave room for self-government. Here is the paradox as it emerges in the mouth of the physicist Niels Bohr (1885–1962), Danish Nobel Prize laureate and one of the principal protagonists in Michael Frayn's award-winning play *Copenhagen*:

> Throughout history we keep finding ourselves displaced. We keep exiling ourselves to the periphery of things. First we turn ourselves into a mere adjunct of God's unknowable purposes, tiny figures in the great cathedral of creation. And no sooner have we recovered ourselves in the Renaissance, no sooner has man become, as Protagoras proclaimed him, the measure of all things, that we're pushed aside again by the products of our own reasoning! We're dwarfed again as physicists build the great new cathedrals for us to wonder at—the laws of classical mechanics that predate us from the beginning of eternity, that will survive us to eternity's end, that exist whether we exist or not. (*Copenhagen*, 71)

But what if we discovered a scientific account of human affairs that made room for individual judgment, discrimination, agency, and hence for freedom? Could science then serve human ends, compromising neither science nor freedom? Quantum mechanics seems to supply a model for such an account of human freedom, since it incorporates the observer's perspective into a general account of reality. In *Copenhagen,* Frayn recreates a controversial and mysterious meeting in 1941 between Niels Bohr and his friend and colleague Werner Heisenberg (1900 1976) both responsible for the development of the so-called Copenhagen interpretation of quantum mechanics—in order to illustrate the curious affinities between human experience and the new science of quantum physics. Thus does Frayn invite his readers and audiences to entertain the possibility of what Heisenberg calls "quantum ethics" (92).

Frayn's invitation, as we shall shortly see, is fraught with considerable difficulties, of which Frayn is himself keenly aware. Unlike those postmodernists who have sought to appropriate quantum physics for nihilistic ends, Frayn does not claim that uncertainty precludes the possibility of attaining knowledge. Determining the limits of human perspective is not the same as asserting that we do not know or cannot know. Rather, quantum mechanics provides a useful framework within which to reflect on the curious space occupied by human beings between ignorance and knowledge. The animating principles of the Copenhagen interpretation—"uncertainty" and "complementarity," about which we will have more to say shortly—seem to express both what we know and don't know about ourselves and each other, as well as the consequences of partial knowledge for moral life. Quantum ethics points toward skepticism, not nihilism, Socrates rather than Nietzsche.

science fiction

Frayn's play does not purport to be history, so we should not read it as such. But it is based on historical evidence, some of which informs the play and sheds light on Frayn's intentions. A provisional overview may be useful. Niels Bohr and Werner Heisenberg's collaborations began in Copenhagen in the mid-1920s, where Bohr was director of the Institute for Theoretical Physics, and Heisenberg a freshly minted Ph.D. from the University of Munich who had just accepted a lectureship at Bohr's institute. It was during Heisenberg's tenure there that the principal ideas which inform the Copenhagen interpretation of quantum mechanics began to surface. In March 1927, Heisenberg submitted his groundbreaking paper describing the "uncertainty principle," while in September of the same year Bohr delivered a conference paper on the "complementarity principle." The former principle expresses the indeterminacy of measurement at the subatomic level: the more I know about a particle's position, the less I know about its momentum, and vice versa. The complementarity principle, on the other hand, states that knowledge of subatomic phenomena requires a description of both its wave- and particle-like properties. Depending on experimental arrangements (these the work of human ingenuity, choice, and judgment), subatomic phenomena are "seen" in either their wave- or particle-like properties, not both simultaneously. Together, these two principles became the essence of the Copenhagen interpretation, which exposed the limitations of Newtonian classical mechanics as a comprehensive understanding of matter.

In October 1927, Heisenberg accepts a professorship in theoretical physics at the University of Leipzig, Germany. And it is his decision to remain in Germany under National Socialism and his willingness to accept a role in the Nazi atomic program that make Heisenberg's 1941 meeting with Bohr in Copenhagen all the more vexed. For at that time the Nazis occupied Denmark. According to Thomas Powers, whose *Heisenberg's War: The Secret History of the German Bomb,* provided Frayn with a historiography on which to base his play, Heisenberg had certainly had opportunities to leave Germany and good reasons for doing so. But not "even an ominous attack on Heisenberg, labeled as a 'white Jew' for his defense of 'Jewish physics,'" writes Powers, "could shake his determination to remain in Germany, come what may. Friends all but begged him to take a job in America in 1939. He refused. He said he felt an obligation to protect his students, share his country's fate and help rebuild German science when the war was over" (ix–x). Powers wonders, as must we: "Did Heisenberg's commitment to his country extend to Hitler and Hitler's war? Would Heisenberg contribute his brain power to the German war effort? Would Heisenberg do what so many of his friends among the allies were doing—work flat out to build an atomic bomb?" (x). As Powers notes, fears that Germany would successfully develop the bomb were not unreasonable: nuclear fission had been discovered in Germany; Germany housed Europe's only uranium mines; and in May 1940, German soldiers seized the world's only heavy-water plant in Norway. So, the question is, in meeting with Bohr, was Heisenberg seeking intelligence about the Allied effort to build the bomb? Or was the intention of the visit less sinister, amounting, perhaps, to an attempt by Heisenberg to allay Bohr's fears about the Nazi bomb program? Or to reestablish their friendship over and above patriotic sentiments and allegiances? Or to seek Bohr's counsel about the use of nuclear weaponry? Frayn's play explores these alternative possibilites.

Copenhagen is not a history. But neither is it a mere fantasy. So what is it? I believe that Frayn's play is itself an illustration of the gap between Word and Flesh. That is, there are limits to what we can say definitively about matter and its constitutive parts. Our perspectives are always partial and hence uncertain. In his "Postscript" to *Copenhagen,* the playwright describes for us Heisenberg's memories in order to show "that science is rooted in conversations." In other words, science is more than the application of a method, more than a series of experiments. It proceeds through all of the vagaries, limitations, possibilities, and complications of common speech. And as we shall later see, this is a problem that mathematics is meant to alleviate but never entirely overcomes. As Frayn's Heisenberg acknowledges, "conversations, even real conversations, cannot be reconstructed literally several decades later" (96). Which is to say that facts, even "scientific" facts, are filtered through the mind, and memory is not an entirely reliable depository. Frayn's Heisenberg therefore gives himself license to recreate those conversations upon which quantum mechanics is based.

Son of a classics professor, and himself an accomplished classicist, Heisenberg endorses the recreation of the past by appealing to the authority of Thucydides. In the preface to the *History of the Peloponnesian War,* reports Frayn, Thucydides tells his readers that he "avoided all 'storytelling,' when it came to the speeches." Yet the Greek historian also admits that it was "impossible to remember their exact wording." As a consequence, says Thucydides, he "made each orator speak as, in my opinion, he would have done in the circumstances, but keeping as close as I could to the train of thought that guided his actual speech." Frayn follows suit. "Some of the dialogue in my play represents speeches that must have been made in one form or another; some of it speeches that were certainly never made at all." Frayn appeals to "the Thucydidean principle . . . that speeches (and indeed actions) follow in so far as possible the original protagonists' train of thought" (97). We can identify with what most likely did transpire, without knowing what actually transpired, by reference to the logic of speech and action. This curious invocation of necessity Frayn justifies by referring to the power of the imagination.

> The great challenge facing the storyteller and the historian alike is to get inside people's heads, to stand where they stood and see the world as they saw it, to make some informed estimate of their motives and intentions—and this is precisely where recorded and recordable history cannot reach. Even when all the external evidence has been mastered, the only way into the protagonists' heads is through the imagination. This indeed is the substance of the play. (97)

This quotation gives us a glimpse of just what a vexed, ironic, perhaps paradoxical play *Copenhagen* is. It is neither to be understood nor to be judged by its fidelity to the so-called facts. Rather, it goes right to the heart of the perennial tension between experience, that which we call fact, and our *account* of experience, that which we call fiction. We are creatures of the Word, of speech, as much as we are creatures of Flesh, or experience. Therefore, the incapacity to provide a complete and final account of experience is as much a problem for the storyteller as it is for the scientist, even when the uncertainties of experience are given the appearance of permanence by the veneer of mathematics. Frayn's play recovers for us the centrality of the storyteller, weaving together metaphors—by their nature ambiguous and indirect—while providing us with imaginative resources to fill the gaps between (or conflate) ourselves and the "other," between "I" and Nature. Recall that quantum mechanics indicates the limitations of human knowing, not the complete impossibility of knowledge. *Copenhagen* is, I suggest, Socratic in nature, for it points us to the truth that wisdom consists in knowledge of our ignorance.

beginning

Copenhagen proceeds by presenting to its audience three "drafts," each an attempt by a different protagonist to understand the meaning of Heisenberg's visit. Each is revealing. Like subatomic particles, the "events" appear to us differently depending on the manner in which we choose to examine them. And they appear differently based on the knowledge we bring to them. The first draft establishes the character of the two principal protagonists, Heisenberg the young mathematical genius and Bohr a fatherly figure attentive to common sense. Their respective devotions to a particular view of nature will erode as we move from draft to draft. By play's end, we will learn why Heisenberg, for whom numbers are "sense," eventually comes to appreciate that "mathematics becomes very odd when you apply it to people" (29), and why Bohr, always mindful of the need to explain science in "plain language," at one crucial moment sees himself in mathematical terms: "I was formed by nature to be a mathematically curious entity: not one but half of two" (29). The erosion of each point of view prepares the ground for Heisenberg's proposal of a "quantum ethics."

We pick up the action during Niels and Werner's reminiscence about their first meeting, which came at Gottingen in 1922 during a "lecture festival" held in Bohr's honor (21). Bohr was feted first, says Heisenberg, as a "great physicist," and "secondly because you were one of the very few people in Europe who were prepared to have dealings with Germany." Even though the Great War had been over for several years, "we were still lepers." "You held out your hand to us then," says Heisenberg to Bohr, "and we took it" (22). Bohr's perspective, and therefore his interpretation, differs. He recalls that after he had delivered a lecture at the festival, Heisenberg had "stood up and laid into me." A mere twenty years old, amidst rows "of eminent physicists and mathematicians, all nodding approval of my benevolence and wisdom," Heisenberg had gotten up to tell "me that my mathematics are wrong" (22). Bohr emerges as the calm, deliberate scientist, respectful of time, tradition, and place, mathematical exactness trumped by what he deems more important considerations, while Heisenberg was, in his view, an impetuous young scientist interested only in the truth as the numbers expressed it.

Frayn's play proceeds to elaborate on this initial distinction. Bohr calls Heisenberg "combative" and compares the German's response to his lecture to a previous game of table tennis. Heisenberg had wanted to win; Bohr had "wanted an agreeable game" (23). Heisenberg counters with his own comparison. "What about those games of poker in the ski-hut at Bayrischzell, then?" During one such game, Bohr had "cleaned us all out" with a "non-existent straight!" All of the mathematicians at the table had been "counting the cards" and were therefore ninety percent certain that Bohr hadn't "got anything," yet Bohr had gone on raising the stakes. "This insane confidence," exclaims the exasperated Heisenberg, had persisted until "our faith in mathematical probability begins to waver, and one by one we all throw in." But Bohr really had thought he had a straight. "I misread the cards! I bluffed myself!" (23). Note that mathematical probability is described in terms of faith. Bohr was wrong, yet at the same time he had got it right, demonstrating even that his opponents' belief in mathematical probability ultimately rested on "faith."

Then there was the skiing at Bayrischzell. The physicists argue over how long it had taken Heisenberg to make it down the hill: was it eight or ten minutes? Bohr supposedly had taken forty-five. They then draw comparisons between skiing and science. Heisenberg weighs in first. "Your skiing was like your science. What were you waiting for? Me and Weizsacker to come back and suggest some slight change of emphasis?" To which Bohr responds, "probably" (24). Bohr had gone down the hill at a rate that allowed him to examine each nook and crevice. "At least I knew where I was," he retorts. "At the speed you were going you were up against the uncertainty relationship. If you knew where you were when you were down you didn't know how fast you'd got there. If you knew how fast you'd been going you didn't know you were down" (24).

Bohr is concerned with topography, the physical terrain, which he examines with great care as he traverses it. He places confidence in the matter as it appears to him and to common sense. This is consistent with his concern for decorum and propriety. He is agreeable, not contentious. Heisenberg, however, with his unwavering faith in numbers, is a Cartesian. Bohr criticizes Heisenberg's mathematical rigor in light of its "real-world" implications. You "never cared what got destroyed on the way . . . As long as the mathematics worked out you were satisfied" (25). Heisenberg agrees with this assessment: "If something works it works"—which is to say that if it works out mathematically it works. For Bohr, on the other hand, "the question is always, What does the mathematics mean, in plain language?" Heisenberg responds: "Decisions make themselves when you're coming downhill at seventy kilometres an hour. Suddenly there's the edge of nothingness in front of you. Swerve left? Swerve right? Or think about it and die? In your head you swerve both ways . . ." (25).

draft two

This first "draft" of the exchange between Bohr and Heisenberg must be considered in light of the second. Frayn's play now makes a new beginning. As before, Bohr, arguing with Heisenberg, insists on the need for common sense. This time, however, he puts common sense in terms of his need to be able to "explain it all to Margrethe," his wife (65). For his part, in this draft Heisenberg raises questions about Bohr's professed empiricism. Heisenberg makes a claim that number-crunching social scientists are fond of making about their craft, namely, that his science is "empirical," the Greek root of which means "experience." To Heisenberg, this is not a perversion of language.

"Mathematics is sense! That's what sense is!" (65). Like our contemporary social scientists, Heisenberg seems to be saying that mathematics is able to attend to phenomena with a kind of precision that eludes common speech. If the task of speech is reasonably to conjoin disparate and seemingly disjointed phenomena, then is not mathematical language the best way of doing so? According to Heisenberg, Bohr fails to appreciate the connection between numbers and things. He is by disposition more attentive to irregularity than to regularity: "You actually loved the paradoxes, that's your problem. You reveled in the contradictions." But Bohr's rejoinder is compelling. "Yes, and you've never been able to understand the suggestiveness of paradox and contradiction. That's your problem. You live and breathe paradox and contradiction, but you can no more see the beauty of them than the fish can see the beauty of the water" (65–66). Heisenberg is faithful to the Cartesian insistence on the sovereignty of method over experience. He is thus blind to that which is perceived by the pre- (or post-)modern Bohr. Each has a distinct way of approaching natural phenomena. Their respective approaches are deeply rooted in their characters, and each has a perspective that the other seems unable to share.

Just when the characters appear as far apart from each other as possible, Frayn initiates a change. In so doing, the characters acquire a new enlightenment about their own and each other's situations that sets the terms for quantum ethics. Bohr's wife Margrethe plays the key role. It is she who draws the two characters together by showing them that they are both animated by personal motives. Margrethe sees what eludes Bohr and Heisenberg, namely, those all-too-human impulses and feelings to which we are all subject: "confusion and rage and jealousy and tears and no one knowing what things mean or which way they're going to go" (73). She chastises Bohr's account of his own understanding of and contributions to science. "I'm sorry, but you want to make everything seem heroically abstract and logical . . . when you tell the story, yes, it all falls into place, it all has a beginning and a middle and an end." Margrethe shows Bohr that for all his love of paradox he abandons neither reason nor logic. Bohr criticizes Heisenberg's attachment to numbers only to put reason in the service of his pride. Turning to Heisenberg, she reminds the German that within "three months of publishing your uncertainty paper" he was offered a position at Leipzig (73). The Copenhagen interpretation served his personal ambitions. Did he not accept the interpretation because he was "becoming a professor [and] wanted a solidly established doctrine to teach?" Or because "you wanted to have your new ideas publicly endorsed by the head of the church in Copenhagen"—that is, Bohr? She returns to her husband. Bohr embraces Heisenberg, she says, "for accepting his doctrines," for recognizing him "as head of the church" (74).

Margrethe's challenge—that science itself is not an impersonal activity, that the two scientists are both proud and ambitious, blind to their own motives—begins to forge an alliance between them. But this is not accomplished before breaking down Heisenberg's pride sufficiently to evoke Bohr's fatherly compassion. An ethical component to the story now emerges. Margrethe presses Heisenberg, accusing him of collaboration with the Nazis, not necessarily as a Nazi sympathizer, but in the service of his proud and misguided ambition to "demonstrate to the Nazis how useful theoretical physics can be," and in order eventually to save the "honour of German science" (75). Margrethe returns to the skiing metaphor, reminding Heisenberg that he skis "too fast for anyone to see where you are." Heisenberg is always "in more than one position at a time, like one of your particles" (75).

Bohr is stunned by his wife's combativeness. "This is so unlike you!" he exclaims (74). Heisenberg proceeds to defend himself. He tells Margrethe that though he worked with the Nazis, one sovereign fact remains: "I didn't build the bomb." This is no puzzle to Margrethe. She claims that the only reason he didn't was because he "didn't understand the physics" (79). There is much that Heisenberg did not understand, he admits, but the crucial issues he did. Or so Heisenberg claims. Margrethe asks for evidence. Heisenberg produces Otto Hahn: "I gave him a reasonably good account of how the bomb had worked" (80). But only, Margrethe reminds him, "[a]fter the event" (80)—that is, after it had been denotated by the U.S. in Japan. Science, too, is retrospective.

Bohr inquires about the account Heisenberg gave Hahn. Specifically, Bohr asks Heisenberg about the critical mass. "That was the most important thing. The amount of material you needed to establish the chain-reaction. Did you tell him the critical mass?" (81). Heisenberg deflects the question by referring Bohr to tapes of the conversations. The Nazis "had microphones everywhere—they were recording everything. Look it up!" Bohr does not relent. "What was the figure you gave him?" Again Heisenberg is evasive: "I forget." But after Bohr becomes even more aggressive, Heisenberg relents: "I said about a ton" (81). Wrong. The mathematician Heisenberg had for some reason failed to calculate the amount of fissionable material needed to create a nuclear weapon. The mathematical prowess for which he was best known had failed him at the most critical time. And the miscalculation is not a small one. "You were twenty times over," says Bohr (81).

It turns out that Heisenberg had not made the calculation himself. Instead, he had relied on those made by "Perrin and Flugge in 1939" (82). Perrin and Flugge, notes Bohr, had made a calculation for natural uranium. "Wheeler and I showed that it was only the 235 that fissioned." Heisenberg had failed to "calculate the figure for pure 235" (82). Heisenberg the mathematician had spent the entire war "believing that it would take not a few kilograms of 235, but a ton or more." He assumed what he should have proven to be the case. He had been, in a way, a man of faith.

At this point Bohr becomes incensed. Anger and sympathy collide. The calm, deliberate, agreeable Bohr, conscious of context and propriety, is now very much like the erratic Heisenberg we saw previously. Bohr now demands mathematical exactness. "Assumed? Assumed? You never assumed things! That's how you got uncertainty, because you rejected our assumptions! You calculated, Heisenberg! You calculated everything! The first thing you did with a problem was the mathematics!" (85). Heisenberg reminds Bohr that the Dane himself had earlier made the very same assumption. Bohr had said, "no one is going to develop a weapon based on nuclear fission" (11). Why, asks Heisenberg, did Bohr not make the calculation himself? Margrethe intervenes on her husband's behalf. "Because he wasn't trying to build a bomb!" (85). Heisenberg seizes the moment. "Yes. Thank you. Because he wasn't trying to build a bomb. I imagine it was the same with me. Because I wasn't trying to build a bomb. Thank you" (85–86). Bohr, reverting back to the game of cards, acknowledges the strange inversion. "So, you bluffed yourself, the way I did at poker with the straight I never had . . ." (86). Even great scientists fall prey to the dark matter of the unconscious.

draft three

Now the third and final draft in Frayn's play. In the previous two versions, Heisenberg and Bohr greet each other amidst doubts. The protagonists also meet amidst their certainties, yet the full range of their motives is hidden from them. Margrethe dislodges each scientist from his limited viewpoint. Uncertainty creeps in. The unconscious is made conscious. The third draft begins with the protagonists on the edge of the abyss. We are repeatedly brought to the limits of reason. "At once the clear purposes inside my head lose all definite shape. The light falls on them and they scatter. . . . How difficult it is to see even what's in front of one's eyes. All we possess is the present, and the present endlessly dissolves into the past," confesses Heisenberg (86). But just when it seems that the very possibility of knowing is lost, awareness emerges about the very nature of their doubt. This is the key revelation of the third draft. The protagonists discover their own and the other's ignorance, and thus come face to face with collective uncertainty. A new way of looking at the universe and each other dawns on them. As we shall see, the new vision does not belong wholly to each protagonist, but neither is the viewpoint wholly another's. This new view of things is not strictly objective, a view somehow detached from the viewer's perspective, but neither it is strictly subjective, a view impenetrable to the eye of another. Here we have the means by which to avoid both radical objectivity and radical subjectivity. Complementarity emerges alongside uncertainty, making visible the contours of a quantum ethics.

The doubts engendered by Margrethe invite Heisenberg to examine himself. "Here I am at the centre of the universe," he says (86), reinforcing the central place occupied by the observer in the quantum view of reality. This time around, however, Heisenberg understands that there is both himself and whoever or whatever it is that sees himself. That is, Heisenberg sees himself, and he sees himself seeing himself. Particle or wave? "I can feel a third smile in the room, very close to me. Could it be the one I suddenly see for a moment in the mirror there? And is the awkward stranger wearing it in any way connected with this presence that I can feel in the room? This all-enveloping, unobserved presence?" (87). Margrethe has a similar perception. "I watch the two smiles in the room, one awkward and ingratiating, the other rapidly fading from incautious warmth to bare politeness. There's also a third smile in the room, I know, unchangingly courteous, I hope, and unchangingly guarded" (87). Bohr, too. "I glance at Margrethe, and for a moment I see what she can see and I can't—myself, and the smile vanishing from my face as poor Heisenberg blunders on" (87).

Seeing myself as a being being seen allows me to consider the perspective of some other who sees me. I have no guarantee that I see exactly what another sees. We remain in the realm of the imagination and uncertainty, skepticism rather than objectivity. Even so, distance from myself sheds light on what I cannot see as long as I fail to detach myself from myself. There is a way out of the insularity of individual perspective.

Thus, Bohr sees that he does not see himself, and in the process begins to see more of himself. By casting a gaze upon himself, he sees what was previously hidden from him. This allows Bohr to sympathize with Heisenberg's blindness. "I look at him looking at me, anxiously, pleadingly, urging me back to the old days, and I see what he sees. And yes—now it comes, now it comes—there's someone missing from the room. He sees me. He sees Margrethe. He doesn't see himself" (87). A collective self-consciousness seems to emerge, somewhere in between light and darkness. "You remember Elsinore? The darkness inside the human soul. . . ?" Heisenberg asks (87). "Who is he, this all-enveloping presence in the darkness?" (88). The Omniscient One?

With their newly acquired awareness, the protagonists go back to the conclusion of the second draft, tempers flaring, each losing sight of themselves and each other, about to plummet into the abyss. Anger again stands in the way of sympathy. Bohr must overcome himself. He proposes a "thought experiment." Let us suppose, he says, "that I don't go flying off into the night. Let's see what happens if instead I remember the paternal role I'm supposed to play. If I stop, and control my anger, and turn to him. And ask him why" (88–89). "Why," asks Bohr, "are you confident that it's going to be so reassuringly difficult to build a bomb with 235? Is it because you've done the calculation?" If this question had been posed in 1941, if the two physicists had been sufficiently composed to entertain the question, Bohr would have enlightened his colleague about diffusion in 235. What would Heisenberg have then done with this knowledge? And what would Bohr have done with knowledge of Heisenberg's knowledge? Would not ample exposure of all their motives and doubts have hastened the development and use of atomic weaponry? Think of the potential evils. "And suddenly a very different and very terrible new world begins to take shape . . ." (89).

The protagonists are stunned both by the prospects of the knowledge they might have had and by the peculiar benefits of *not* having some knowledge. In short, they are struck by the moral benefits of uncertainty. Margrethe offers a poignant exclamation on behalf of her husband: "That was the last and greatest demand that Heisenberg made on his friendship with you. To be understood when he couldn't understand himself. And that was the last and greatest act of friendship for Heisenberg that you performed in return. To leave him misunderstood" (89).

Knowledge of ignorance opens the way for additional knowledge. Bohr's act of friendship may have been reciprocated on the dreaded night the Nazis came to round up the eight thousand or so Danish Jews: did a tip from the German embassy permit the Bohrs and their fellow Danes to escape? After the Bohrs departed Copenhagen, Heisenberg came back to the institute there. "You know they offered me your cyclotron?" Heisenberg asks Bohr rhetorically (91). While Heisenberg was going back to Copenhagen, Bohr was on his way from "Sweden to Los Alamos," where, as Bohr himself admits, he would "play my small but helpful part in the deaths of a hundred thousand people," whereas, continues Bohr, "you, my dear Heisenberg, never managed to contribute to the death of one single solitary person in all your life" (90).

hamlet's soul

This might seem a fitting end to the play. We have before us a poignant reminder of the dangers of knowledge. To this point, the play has invited us to reconsider the ideologue's call to arms, which, to paraphrase Marx, holds that the purpose of philosophy is not to interpret the world but to change it. For all that separates them, the founders of the new "science of politics" (that is, Bacon, Descartes, Hobbes, Locke) were animated by a spirit akin to Marx's, a devotion to Machiavelli's "effectual truth of the matter." For the moderns, what is true is what works; there is therefore no longer a gap between theory and praxis. But as Bohr's last remark indicates, *Copenhagen* invites a different assessment of the proper relationship between theory and practice. The Nazis heaped scorn on "Jewish physics" because it was "theoretical"; they sought instead to pursue what was thought to be "practical" or applied physics. Yet it turned out that it was the so-called theoreticians who discovered how to use atomic physics for weaponry, while those devoted to "practice" failed to do so. Before us is an instance in which uncertainty, paradoxically, makes possible the unity of thought and practice. Uncertainty is a kind of knowledge, in other words. A certain kind of skepticism, ironically, leads us toward the truth.

Let us return to the scene in which Bohr acknowledges that he departed Copenhagen to work at Los Alamos, where he contributed to the making of the atom bomb. Heisenberg, in spite of his association with the Nazis and his loyalties to his homeland, did not develop and use atomic weaponry. It is again left to Margrethe to flesh out what is left implicit in this strange turn of events. She reminds Heisenberg that he *was* responsible for a death—"One. Or so you told us. The poor fellow you guarded overnight, when you were a boy in Munich, while he was waiting to be shot in the morning" (91). Bohr remembers, too. "All right then, one. One single soul on his conscience, to set against all the others." Margrethe takes offense at Bohr's mathematics. "But that one single soul was emperor of the universe, no less than each of us. Until the morning came" (91). In other words, if we are going to take individual perspective seriously, Bohr's inverted utilitarian calculus, "the least harm to the least number," will not absolve Heisenberg. In his defense, Heisenberg reveals that he eventually persuaded the guards to let the captured boy go. Heisenberg both detained the boy and engineered his release. Which of the two Heisenbergs do we judge? "Heisenberg, I have to say," notes Bohr, "if people are to be measured strictly in terms of observable quantities . . ." (92).

Heisenberg takes it from here, delivering the longest and most intricate speech in the play, beginning with the first and only reference to "quantum ethics." "Then," says Heisenberg, completing Bohr's conditional sentence, "we should need a strange new quantum ethics" (92). Quantum ethics would seem to require a "place in heaven for me." That is, had we seen Heisenberg when he released the detained boy, not knowing where he had previously been, or what he had previously done, we might assign him a place in Heaven. But there are other Heisenbergs to consider, in different spaces and times. What of the Heisenberg who detained the boy? Do we condemn him to hell? The constraints of individual perspective being what they are, how do we render a final verdict on Heisenberg? Omniscience is not ours.

Whether this observable act of goodness (releasing the boy) merits a place for Heisenberg in Heaven is a question that Frayn asks us to entertain in the context of Heisenberg's long speech about a meeting between him and an SS man on his way to Haigerloch near "the end of my war" (92). Before us, in the person of the SS officer, is the personification of evil. We are asked to make a judgment. What do we do with what we know and do not know? Frayn, speaking for Heisenberg, deserves to be heard at length.

> The Allied troops were closing in; there was nothing more we could do. Elisabeth and the children had taken refuge in a village in Bavaria, so I went to see them before I was captured. I had to go by bicycle—there were no trains or road transport by that time—and I had to travel by night and sleep under a hedge by day, because all through the daylight hours the skies were full of Allied planes, scouring the roads for anything that moved. A man on a bicycle would have been the biggest target left in Germany. Three days and three nights I travelled. Out of Wurttemberg, down through Swabian Jura and the first foothills of the Alps. Across my ruined homeland. Was this what I'd chosen for it? This endless rubble? This perpetual smoke in the sky? These hungry faces? Was this my doing? And all the desperate people on the roads. The most desperate of all were the SS. Bands of fanatics with nothing left to lose, roaming around shooting deserters out of hand, hanging them from roadside trees. The second night, and suddenly there it is—the terrible familiar black tunic emerging from the twilight in front of me. On his lips as I stop—the one terrible familiar word. "Deserter," he says. He sounds as exhausted as I am. I give him the travel order I've written for myself. But there's hardly enough light

in the sky to read by, and he's too weary to bother. He begins
to open his holster instead. He's going to shoot me because it's
simply less labor. And suddenly I'm thinking very quickly and
clearly—it's like skiing, or that night on Heligoland, or the one
in Faelled Park. What comes into my mind this time is the pack
of American cigarettes I've got in my pocket. And already it's in
my hand—I'm holding it out to him. The most desperate solution to a problem yet. I wait while he stands there looking at it,
trying to make it out, trying to think, his left hand holding my
useless piece of paper, his right hand on the fastening of the
holster. There are two simple words in large print on the pack:
Lucky Strike. He closes his holster, and takes the cigarettes instead. . . . It had worked, it had worked! Like all the other solutions to all the other problems. For twenty cigarettes he let me
live. And on I went. . . . (92–93)

Heisenberg has come to realize that our lives are not con-
trolled experiments, where we isolate variables, or keep this
or that constant, all under the benefits of an artificial environment. We are not even fully self conscious. Our motives as well
as others' do not ever come into the full light of day. This does
not render human agency null and void. There are choices to
make. We are all, however, constrained by time, circumstance,
history, and the unequal endowments of nature. Frayn notes
that Fortuna will make her appearance whether we are certain
or uncertain. Frayn also returns us to Heisenberg's earlier statement about the character of decision-making. To repeat: "Decisions make themselves when you're coming downhill at seventy
kilometres an hour. Suddenly there's the edge of nothingness in
front of you. Swerve left? Swerve right? Or think about it and
die? In your head you swerve both ways . . ." (27). Each time

one of Frayn's characters bumps into the limits of reason, some strange voice or force emerges that helps render a judgment. Which is to say: for all of the deliberation we engage in to ensure that our choices are reasonably sound, how many times do we resort to intuition? Conscience? To that which is subconscious? And what is the relationship between our deliberations and that final act of the will? How do we make determinations about others and ourselves when we are as others partially hidden in the darkness? Would this mean that there is no "science" of human affairs, not even a quantum ethics? How deep does skepticism go?

There are no unequivocal and certain answers to these questions. But Frayn is cryptically suggestive. Consider, for example, a discussion between Bohr and Heisenberg on the release of atomic energy. "You fire a neutron at a uranium nucleus, it splits, and it releases energy," says Bohr (33). Initially, the amount of energy released is small, "enough to move a speck of dust." But as two or three more neutrons are released, each "has the chance of splitting another nucleus." And consequently, you start a chain reaction, an "ever-widening chain of split nuclei forks through the uranium, doubling and quadrupling in millionths of a second from one generation to the next." But "there is a catch," interjects Heisenberg. "There is a catch, thank God," Bohr adds. "Natural uranium consists of two different isotopes, U-238 and U-235. Less than one percent of it is U-235, and this tiny fraction is the only part of it that's fissionable by fast neutrons." There is a "double catch," Bohr continues (34). U-238 "is not only impossible to fission by fast neutrons—it also absorbs them. So, very soon after the chain reaction starts, there aren't enough fast neutrons left to fission the 235." Not only would there be a need for large amounts of pure 235 to make the long chain reaction necessary for a large explosion, the effort to separate it is, in Bohr's words, "mercifully difficult." Mercy intervenes to thwart human ingenuity (34).

There are other instances in which the Promethean-like propensities of human beings to tamper with and harness the forces of nature are foiled by cosmic limits or human error. Frayn implies that we should be thankful for this. He also implies that it may be no accident.

Consider the characters' many references to God and Christianity. Throughout the play Frayn puts into the mouths of his protagonists references to "John the Baptist" (7), to Bohr as "Pope" (39, 56, 60, and 64), to Heisenberg's "cardinal" (58), and to "papal progress" (59 and 67); we are led to believe that Heisenberg comes to Copenhagen in search of "absolution" (39); that we are given dreams only God fully understands (7 and 45); that scientists make "spiritual" rather than simply practical contributions to humanity (47); that the protagonists prosecute their scientific principles with "religious fervor" (70); that Heisenberg's life is a "windowless hell" (66); that he is the prodigal son (53–54). What do we make of a God of negation, a sympathetic God who withholds more than he gives, present more in the dark than in the light? What is "dark matter"? In two stark occasions we are reminded that Bohr and Margrethe's son, with the significant name of Christian, drowned in an accident (29–30 and 53–54). Yet, according to the play, there was also a brief moment in time when the Bohrs found themselves "free of all the dark tangled currents in the water" (54). Whether that moment persists, and if there is any refuge in it, I leave the wise reader to decide.

Beyond the Edge of Reason

*And science itself, our science—what indeed is
the meaning of all science, viewed as a symptom
of life? What is the purpose, and, worse still, what
is the origin of all science? What? Is scientific
method perhaps no more than fear of and flight
from pessimism? A subtle defense against truth?*
— Friedrich Nietzsche

Coldplay is unquestionably among the biggest bands in the world, and much of their popularity derives from the fact that they sing so beguilingly about the predicament that afflicts us as children of the modern world. Coldplay realizes—and exploits to great effect—that the culture of modernity has been powered by great scientific and technological discoveries that have provided us with a variety of necessary and not-so-necessary goods, and that all of this dynamism has an ugly side. Our employment of powerful technologies has, for one thing, depleted nature, and we instinctually rebel at the idea that forests, ice-covered lands, rivers, mountains, oceans, and seas are nothing more than "resources" intended for our use. The human constructions and destructions characteristic of modernity therefore lead to ambivalence. We live by, as well as doubt, progress. We are no longer sure if technology can save us from technology. The so-called authentic and genuine eludes us. We feel increasingly artificial. Human attachments seem fleeting. We yearn for permanence in a world of flux. And yet who can deny the obvious benefits of science? Coldplay sings this dilemma.

Coldplay comprises vocalist Chris Martin, Jonny Buckland, Guy Berryman, and Will Champion. Martin and Buckland met in 1996 while students at University College, London. Berry and Champion joined shortly thereafter. The four became Coldplay in 1998. Martin is the principal lyricist and, arguably, the group's mastermind. The principal themes running through Coldplay's lyrics appear in their first major release, *Parachutes,* which opens with the admonition "Don't Panic." We have reason to panic, it seems, because we live in a "beautiful world," yet do not know how to square the feelings evoked by beauty in the cosmos with the fear evoked by our position in the cosmos. "Bones, sinking like stones . . . All of us are done for," Coldplay tells us. In the face of despair we find solace, in that "everybody here's got somebody to lean on." But these interludes prove fleeting.

From panic we move to "Shiver," which tells us that the universe is a cold and lonely place. Then from "Shiver" to "Spies." (The titles alone are revealing.) Answers are not forthcoming. The universe is constructed in a way that makes appearances deceiving. In a deceptive universe, "I awake to find no peace of mind." Home is not home. "How do you live as a fugitive?" We run but we are not sure from whom, or what, or to what end. "Down here where I cannot see so clear / I said what do I know? / Show me the right way to go." From the singular we move to the plural: the predicament is universal. "I awake to see that no one is free / We're all fugitives, look at the way we live / Down here, I cannot sleep from fear, no. . . . I said which way do I turn? / I forget everything I learn." We are all both fugitives and captives—fugitives and captives who suspect the existence of spies, which adds an especially ominous character to our oppression. Are we watched from above, below, or by each other? Who is the warden?

Coldplay weaves its stories with and within the four basic elements: earth, air, fire, and water. These basic elements represent different psychological states, and the division of the universe and of souls into these categories allows Coldplay to approach problems of integration. Is water the opposite of fire, earth the opposite of air? Then how do they work together? Are we at odds with ourselves? In "Trouble," for example, the band refers to "a spider web" that "is tangled up with me." There follows an attempt by the narrator to reason his way out of his troubles, but this proves fruitless. "I lost my head," he laments. To seek a way "out" or at least a measure of control is a consistent theme for the group. In "High Speed" Coldplay asks: "Can anybody stop this thing? / Before my head explodes, / Or my head starts to ring?" Not really; there is only the momentary solace to be found in the presence of another. "Confidence in you / Is confidence in me."

"We Never Change" follows "High Speed." Here the singer-protagonist wants to "live life" and "never be cruel." He wants to be "good to you," yet knows that "we never change do we no, no." The genetic flaw that thwarts the effort to overcome oneself is put in a theological context: "Yes and I sin every single day." Chris Martin and his wife Gwyneth Paltrow even decided to name their first child Apple and their second Moses—not exactly common names. Why choose these biblical references, then, the first alluding to the primordial vehicle of original sin and the second to a captive people seeking the Promised Land? Coldplay frames its despair in biblical terms only to argue for the insufficiency of the biblical view. In "Everything's Not Lost," they imply that our kinship is with the demonic. "When I counted up my demons, / Saw there was one for every day." So if you "ever feel neglected, / And if you think that all is lost / I'll be counting up my demons, yeah, / Hoping everything's not lost."

the science of love

What is muted in *Parachutes* becomes front and center in *A Rush of Blood to the Head* (*RBH*) and is then dissipated and transformed in Coldplay's third album *x and y*. Let us begin with *RBH*'s clever and revealing cover, which features an image of a person beginning at the chest and with about one half of the head missing. The heart seems also to be missing, while streaks emerging from the back of the head suggest that the severed head is in motion, or perhaps has been caught by something in movement that has removed everything from the mouth up. Before us, then, is a person with no brain, no eyes, and no heart. Part of an ear *is* depicted, however, so that the only visible sense organs are those principally connected with the fabrication of sound and the ingestion of food. Is this ravaged body intended to be a portrayal of our appetites? Or could this be a depiction of the consequences of thought? Or thoughtlessness?

Insert a recent Coldplay DVD and up pops the same image. Now it is clearer and in motion. The image seems to be constructed by triangles, a web of lines and shapes. The web appears to consist of electrons in motion. If you recently attended a Coldplay concert, you will recognize the web as human skin. Look at the geometrical configurations on the back of your hand. Look at them under a microscope. Like Gulliver, Coldplay sees the world through both a microscope and a telescope. What's in between those two worlds poses the greatest challenge. A similar web of lines and shapes seems to encase the image. Click on "Extras" and the image dissolves. Reconstituted, the streaks behind the head come into focus, giving us a partial but clearer image. Click on "Tour Diary" and you find a globe, a bright speck of light in the center, a smaller globe around it, and another larger globe around that. The figure is geometric, lines that form a circle and give the appearance of another atom in motion. The image is not entirely self-contained; its edges fade into the black background. All of these images are presented in black and white. To find color, we click on "Tour," whereupon the image dissolves yet again, is reconstituted in squares, within them the band performing amidst vivid color and bright lights. Keep colors, circles, and squares as well as these competing perspectives in mind as we reflect on the movement from *RBH* to *x and y*.

Much like *Parachutes, RBH*'s theme is homelessness. The first song, "Politik," asks us to "Look at earth from outer space / Everyone must find a place / Give me time and give me space

/ Give me real, don't give me fake." Looking at the world from outer space does not, of course, evoke feelings of belonging. That is not where we live. Our human perspective takes shape on earth in the context of family, town, city, and nation. We are lovers, fathers and mothers, sons and daughters, practicing our various vocations or employments, obeying the laws of the land when we can't get away with doing otherwise. To be sure, a view of the earth without its various human divisions, races, creeds, and cultures speaks to our universal and democratic aspirations. But space is cold and inhospitable. In the face of the abstraction before us the singer-poet asks for "strength, reserve, control." Yet he also seeks "heart" and "soul."

"In My Place" is the appropriate follow up. "In my place, in my place, / Were lines that I couldn't change, / I was lost. . . ." The singer-poet may have an assigned place, but it does not seem to provide fully for his human needs and hopes. Curiously, he is both in a circumscribed space and yet lost. A bit like being free yet bound. Is this what it means to be a fugitive? Simultaneously chained and lost, the singer feels the need to transgress established boundaries. "I was lost, I was lost, / Crossed lines I shouldn't have crossed." Not all transgressions deliver on the promise of freedom, and they come with costs. "Yeah, how long must you wait for it? / Yeah, how long must you pay for it?" The protagonist is left with nothing but song, or rather a longing for song: "Sing it please, please, please."

These cosmic and contradictory hopes for freedom and home are bound to evoke thoughts about one's Maker. Who or what put this all together? Accordingly, the next song is "God Put a Smile Upon Your Face." Yet when contemplating the biblical God, Coldplay asserts his insufficiency. "Where do we go, nobody knows / I've got to say I'm on my way down / God give me style and give me grace / God put a smile upon my face." But if God puts a smile on our face in the midst of our loneliness, homelessness, and confusion, we have reason to reconsider the nature of that smile. When we do so, the smile looks more like a sneer. It prompts a desire to reject God's grace. "Where do we go to draw the line / I've got to say I wasted all your time / Oh honey honey / Where do I go to fall from grace." This rejection, though, is filled with ambivalence: when "you work it out I'm worse than you." We envy those who seem to have been blessed with grace. And in the modern world, we wonder what would even constitute a sign of grace. "God gave you style and gave you grace . . . when you work it out I want it too." Must we have *style* along with grace? What we once held dear is evacuated of all meaning.

This journey prepares us for what I take to be Coldplay's best and, in some ways, their most compelling song, "The Scientist." Making explicit the problems, contradictions, and shortcomings of our "politik," Coldplay invites us to consider a new beginning. "The Scientist" begins, as most creation stories do, with a transgression. Beginning at beginnings is part of Coldplay's stratagem. "Come up to meet you, tell you I'm sorry / You don't know how lovely you are." We do not know the nature of the transgression, but it demands redress. The singer-poet feels impelled to let the transgressed know that he or she is lovely. (As in Eden, sin is mixed with beauty. The fruit is lovely to look at.) Whatever the reparations may be, they are not offered for the purposes of reconciliation. "I had to find you / Tell you I need you / Tell you I set you apart." Thus is the desire for unity coupled with the desire for singularity. We want to be ourselves—special, unique, and individual—but we want also to be a part of some larger collective, whether human or natural (or both), that lifts us beyond ourselves. Is this contradiction part of some God's twisted logic?

The picture is not entirely bleak. Coldplay told us as early as "Spies" that something is being withheld from us. Ignorance, however, is not satisfying. "Tell me your secrets / And ask me your questions / Oh let's go back to the start." By entertaining the questions of another we may find answers—one of the lessons of *Copenhagen.* Questions compound questioning, and there is no indication that answers are forthcoming. We live in a world of chance: "Running in circles / Coming up tails / Heads on the silence apart." Even science cannnot discover more than cosmic silence. The reference to "tails" also deserves notice. More than chance is implied here. We will shortly have occasion to attend to the evolutionary themes running through Coldplay's music.

If we could somehow go back to the beginning of time, of the cosmos, either hypothetically or imaginatively (after all there are no eyewitnesses), we might discover an essence, a purpose perhaps, or an initial impetus that could explain what we are and why we are here. "Nobody said it was easy," true, but an interesting play on words follows this acknowledged difficulty: "Oh it's such a shame for us to part." Now, when we say "apart," we refer to separation. But separate the word into the indefinite article and the noun, and we get "a part," which often refers to a kind of unity, as when we claim to be "a part" of something or someone. (Coldplay is infatuated with the word "part" and with the mysteries of language generally.)

The second half of the song moves from the personal to the universal. Its structure is now predictable. Coldplay sings about

and to us all. Autobiography alone will not explain and elu-
cidate. Again the universal is couched in scientific language.
"I was just guessing / At numbers and figures / Pulling the
puzzles apart." Science seems to befuddle. However, Coldplay
is not wholeheartedly an enemy of science. The puzzles of life
are also the puzzles of science. Science provides a window into
what we are—but one does not see *everything* through that window. "Questions of science / Science and progress / Do not
speak as loud as my heart." Note, though, that the questions
of science and progress still speak, and to be louder does not
necessarily mean to be more compelling. Confusion persists.
"Running in circles / Chasing our tails / Coming back as we
are." The coccyx is a vestige of what we were. But this ape,
homo sapiens, has reason and speech. Are the limitations of instinct the limitations of the heart? Bewildered, our protagonist
reaches out for love, again. "Tell me you love me / Come back
and haunt me / Oh and I rush to the start."

time

Throughout *RBH,* Coldplay meditates on our precarious individuality as we move aimlessly in a wonderful, awful, beautiful, horrible, and terrifying universe. The next song, "Clocks,"
takes this meditation one step further. Here our individuality is
considered in the context of time. We are beings of and in time,
yet with the capacity to think beyond time, both backwards and
forwards, eternity and death rolled into one. There are ends
to beginnings, beginnings to ends. This meditation on time is
prompted by a despair that Coldplay seems unable to shake.
"The lights go out and I can't be saved / Tides that I tried to

swim against / Have brought me down upon my knees / Oh I beg, I beg and plead singing." Beg for what? Salvation? It is no mere coincidence that this depiction of our struggle in time is followed by a reference to William Tell—that icon of rebellion and freedom, the man who thought it justifiable to kill a tyrant who demands inhumane acts. "Come out of things unsaid / Shoot an apple off my head and a / Trouble that can't be named / A tiger's waiting to be tamed singing." The next two lines cry out, "You are / You are." Am I a part of the architect's plan? "Confusion never stops / Closing walls and ticking clocks." In the face of cosmic hostility, there is again a familiar glimmer of hope. "Gonna come back and take you home / I could not stop that you now know singing." "Daylight" (which follows "Clocks") also seems to provide a temporary respite. "To my surprise / And my delight / I saw a sunrise / I saw a sunlight." After all, "I am nothing / In the dark." Our singer delights in the light. Enlightenment now serves our needs. "On a hilltop / On a sky-rise / Like a first born / Child." We are reborn. "And at full tilt / And in full flight / Defeat darkness / Breaking daylight." The song concludes with the words "Slowly breaking through the daylight" repeated ten times.

The birthing metaphor used in "Daylight" is employed in the final three songs of the album. "A Whisper," another song about time, opens with "A whisper, a whisper, a whisper, a whisper" for a total of eight times. The whisper is coincident with, or is itself, "the sound of the ticking of clocks." There is no permanent, enduring resting place in Coldplay's vision. Nothing is eternal save the passage of time and of all things in time. "Who remembers your face / Who remembers you when you are gone." Light is not salvation. "Night turns to day /

And I still have these questions / Bridges will break / Should I go forwards or backwards / Night turns to day / And I still get no answers." Coldplay repeatedly speaks of going forward and backward, and they enact their obsession. Consider the videos for "The Scientist" and "fix you" (from *x and y*). The singer-poet is in reverse, yet the words come in their proper sequence. Forward or backward but to no end; there is no bearable present save in love. And then we die. And the crowds continue to gather for each concert.

We come now to the title song of Coldplay's second album. "A Rush of Blood to the Head" is predictable given the predicament Coldplay depicts as coeval with the human situation. Destruction, death, and, at the conclusion of the album—suicide. As if to moderate the morbid suggestions of "A Rush of Blood to the Head," Coldplay does not at first use first-person narration. "*He said* I'm gonna buy this place and burn it down / I'm gonna put it six feet underground / *He said* I'm gonna buy this place and watch it fall / Stand here beside me baby in the crumbling walls" (emphases mine). But suddenly that "he said" disappears. As if in the singer-poet's own voice, we learn that violence is precipitated by revenge: "Do back the things it did to you in return." Again, a transgression. But before revenge we hear either laughter or a sigh: "Ah ah ah ah ah ah." This is ominous. It is one thing to say that the world is a confusing place. It is another to say that it is absurd. The proper response to the absurd is not reason but ridicule. But how hardy is the laugh? "He said I'm gonna buy a gun and start a war / If you can tell me something worth fighting for." Anger is precipitated by meaninglessness, but it cannot be justified by meaninglessness. "All the movements you're starting to make /

See me crumble and fall on my face / And I know the mistakes that I made / See it all disappear without a trace." Mistakes are acknowledged but not without shifting the blame. How Edenic. "Oh and I'm gonna buy this place that's what I said / Blame it on a rush of blood to the head." We are not responsible for our irresponsibility.

Finally, in the concluding track, "Amsterdam," the protagonist casts another gaze up to the heavens. This time he notices that his "star is fading," and he swerves "out of control." He finds himself at the end of life and thus at the end of time, burdened with memories, regrets, and an impotence borne of lost opportunities. "If I, If I'd only waited / I'd not be stuck here in this hole." There was hope once. "And I swear I waited and waited." Now a call to action. "I've got to get out of this hole." But this call to action is not for the singer, but for his progeny. "But time is on your side / It's on your side now / Not pushing you down and all around / It's no cause for concern." Coldplay sings to another about their despair and then reminds the other that he or she is blessed with time and can therefore afford to be carefree. "Come on, oh my star is fading / And I see no chance of release / I know I'm dead on the surface / But I am screaming underneath." As for the singer himself? He is going to end it all. "Stuck on the end of this ball and chain / And I'm on my way back down again / Stood on a bridge, tied to a noose / Sick to the stomach / You can say what you mean / But it won't change a thing / I'm sick of the secrets." Love comes to the rescue. "Stood on the edge / Tied to a noose / You came along / And you cut me loose." But how credible is this rescue in the context of the larger story that has now unfolded through two albums?

the flesh made word

At first glance, *x and y* looks like an attempt to work through some of the conundrums that riddle the previous two albums. But first glances do not tell the whole story. In a highly tentative effort to project hopefulness, we here find Coldplay transforming the puzzles of despair, extending the operative scientific metaphor beyond geometric figures, and finding solace in songs, poems, and words. In *x and y* there is a concentrated effort to get at the meaning of meaninglessness, to capture in intelligible speech that which defies all speech, including song.

We begin at the beginning, again. Set aside capital letters. "square one" begins at "the top of the first page," and then again on "the first line on the first page." The book referred to in the song is scientific but not exclusively geometric. The absence of capitals means that no word is given prominence, and this includes the first word of each sentence. This practice reveals a closer affinity to the idea of the eternal return than to the Judeo-Christian (and perhaps scientific) idea of a world with a beginning and end. "under the surface trying to break through / deciphering the codes in you / i need a compass draw me a map / i'm on the top, i can't get back." What does going below the surface mean, in the context of science? The album cover is revealing. We need not delve into the system devised by Émile Baudot in 1870 that is represented on the cover; the work of solving that not-so-mysterious mystery should be left to the reader. Let us approach the cover by appearances only. When I ask my students what the cover and inserts amount to, they tend to speak of spectra and DNA. Welcome to the genome. Is the meaning of life to be found in that code?

For Coldplay, the search remains for "heart" and "soul," that which is prior to the material world or at least coincident with it. This means that the search Coldplay describes is moral. It cannot be confined to the so-called objective universe of science. We want both facts and values. But the opening of the next song, "what if?" seems to reject the dual nature of the quest. Capital letters return. "What if there was no light / Nothing wrong, nothing right / What if there was no time / And no reason, or rhyme." Nihilism is a reasonable alternative in a world devoid of reason. The possibility of losing the lovely savior is now forcefully present. "What if you should decide / That you don't want me there by your side." Doubts extend. "What if I got it wrong / And no poem or song / Could put right what I got wrong / Or make you feel I belong." Consider the intervention of poetry following the introduction of books. By its very nature, poetry—its reason and rhyme—serves as an intermediary between prose and music. There are gaps in human understanding that we can only fill with our imagination. But not all that we imagine can or should be done. Coldplay vacillates between the desire not to know, or forgetfulness, and the desire to know, or memory.

The confusion in which we find ourselves is curiously situated in systems. Systems seem to provide us with a place, a map. However, we cannot locate ourselves within them. It is not clear where we came from or where we are supposed to go. Hope persists nonetheless: to be "in a permanent state" is a longing expressed in the next song, "white shadows," in which we hear that "we're part of the human race / all of the stars and the outer space / part of the system plan." Childhood innocence is desirable in the face of an overwhelming and paralyzing enlightenment. But this is no counsel to innocence. Recovering childhood provides us with a new opportunity to come to terms with the universe in ways that our current understanding subverts or thwarts: "when I was a young boy I tried to listen / don't you want to feel like that." Perhaps there are other systems that capture the universe by doing justice to our spiritual longings: "little white shadows blink and miss them / part of a system, I am." The seas return as a symbol for humanity: "swim out on a sea of faces / tide of the human races / an answer now is what I need. . . ." The dawn holds out promise: "see it in a new sun rising / see it break on your horizon / come on love, stay with me. . . ."

Systems evoke machines. In the marvelously clever song "fix you," a person represents a vehicle, and a vehicle a person. The human as machine, the machine as human. Instead of thinking of our predicament in light of an original transgression, which requires a transnatural redress, better to think of it in terms of a machine that can be repaired, says Coldplay. We are "stuck in reverse," they sing. However, Coldplay also laments the conflation of human and machine, and they seek a way to humanize their world in the face of the fading distinction between the two: "and the tears come streaming down your face / when you lose something you can't replace / when you love someone but it goes to waste / could it be worse?" Tears are from, and for, humans. Now machine and flesh come together: "lights will guide you home / and ignite your bones / and I will try to fix you." What do we make of a body shop run by a mechanic with torch in hand ready for ignition? Are we machines amenable to this kind of repair? We are then told that life as it is meant to be can only be purchased by a death to what we crave, including life itself: "high up above or down below / when you're too in love to let it go / but if you never try you'll never know / just what you're worth." The idea of fixing things also carries over to the song "x and y": "when something is broken / and you try to fix it / trying to repair it / anyway you can." Sea and sky return also as primordial elements of our human world: "you and me are floating on a tidal wave together / you and me are drifting into outer space"—all the while, of course, "singing."

before the beginning, or till kingdom come

The song "speed of sound" follows "x and y." Here Coldplay tries to penetrate the various barriers to perception and deception. We are no longer at the beginning. We journey prior to the beginning. Let us take a step back from something to nothing. Nihilism is again on the horizon—or maybe not. The biblical God is said to create *ex nihilo,* out of nothing. We emerge from the great Void only to find no peace of mind: "where to, where do I go?" Our gaze at heaven now comes from the forest canopy: "look up I look up at night / planets are moving at the speed of light / climb up up in the trees." It is fitting, we discover, that the idea of "the speed of light" emerges in the context of a song supposedly about the speed of sound. What happens to time at the speed of light? Think *Copenhagen.*

Coldplay's meaning here becomes clearer in the video for "speed of sound." We begin with music, a song, emerging out of the darkness. We then see a partially obscured Chris Martin singing, as if alone. Words. The light of dawn or dusk emerges in the background. Then points of light, like stars. A meteor shower follows. The whole scene is configured to produce a mechanized feel. Machine and nature are conjoined. A sun-like brightness emerges behind the screen that drowns out the pyrotechnics. Light blinds no less than darkness. We begin to feel overpowered by the lights and sounds. The images get distorted. We glimpse the musicians at and through different angles. Dazzled, we end with the same dawn dusk light enveloping the blurred and darkened figures of the four band members in the foreground. Fade to black.

The confusion portrayed in this video is echoed in the chorus: "all that noise / and all that sound / all those places I got found." Nature offers some messages, spies and secrets everywhere: "and birds go flying at the speed of sound / to show you how it all began / birds came flying from the underground / if you could see it then you'd understand." This evolutionary theme emerges most clearly in x and y. Consider the program sold and circulated at the "Twisted Logic" tour. On one page we see Chris walking like a chimpanzee, followed thereafter by each of his bandmates at a different stage of evolution: on two feet but still hunched over; on two feet and almost erect; on two feet, fully erect and reading a newspaper. The program as a whole is a confusing and disjointed plan, if you will pardon the contradiction. It includes blueprints, a copy of Chris's notes, and other images that taken together produce the feeling that we are walking into a human construction site, Coldplay not God presiding. All of this is seen but not quite understood: "ideas that you'll never find / all the inventors could never design / the buildings that you put up / Japan and China all lit up / a sign that I couldn't read / or a light that I couldn't see / some things you have to believe / but others are puzzles, puzzling me." The repeated negations are revealing. We arrive at the other side, briefly: "all those signs I knew what they meant / some things you can't invent / some get made, and some get sent. . . ." Coldplay ends up just where you'd expect. The first line of the next song, "a message," reads: "my song is love."

One gets the feeling Coldplay now has nowhere to go. Its themes are overwrought. Perhaps we wait "Til Kingdom Come," the title of a song the band originally wrote for Johnny Cash and now sings as a tribute to the man in black (Coldplay also dresses in black). This track echoes "The Man Comes Around" from the country singer's *American IV* album. There Cash reflects on the end: "Til Armageddon, no Shalam, no Shalom / Then the father hen will call his chickens home / The wise men will bow down before the thrown / And at his feet they'll cast their golden crown / When the man comes around." But it is not clear that Cash is paying homage to the Lord and to his final verdict: "Whoever is unjust, let him be unjust still. / Whoever is righteous, let him be righteous still. / Whoever is filthy, let him be filthy still / Listen to the words long written down, When the man comes around." Despite all their ambivalence, we should finally not be surprised that on Coldplay's reading, Cash is admired for his defiance: "In your tears . . . and in your blood / In your fire . . . and in your flood / I hear you laugh . . . I heard you sing / I wouldn't change a single thing."

Part Two

Theology

Crown of Thorns

Wagner's music is better than it sounds.
— Mark Twain

Dave Matthews is engaged in a protracted struggle to come to terms with our conflicted and contradictory nature, animated by a belief that we suffer partly because we embrace the perplexing image of the crucifixion as emblematic of a provident and loving God. The crucifixion is the focal point of each of Matthews's numerous albums. As we move through Matthews's compositions, we will discover an evolution (as I think he would call it). It takes Matthews several albums to arrive at and then confront Jesus directly. He descends deeply and calls forth the mysterious forces in our dark souls in his struggle against God. So mighty is the struggle that Matthews finds himself in alliance with none other than the Devil itself. (Indeed, *Some Devil* is the title of Matthews's solo album.) By the time we arrive at *Stand Up,* Matthews tells us that "the serpent, not God pours through my veins" ("Hello Again").

Matthews's starting point is, as it is for believers, original sin. The so-called Fall makes the crucifixion necessary. In "What Would You Say" (*Under the Table and Dreaming*) Matthews makes his inner conflict known: "Up and down the puppies' hair / Fleas and ticks jump everywhere / 'Cause of original sin." He approaches primal stories as a storyteller who understands the power of stories as stories. So he retells these primal stories by drawing from our own reservoir of narratives, nursery rhymes, and fairy tales—the means by which our moral sensibilities are given form and substance. He meets one grand metaphor with a series of lesser ones that gain power by repetition. By evoking memory, he taps into the sounds and images that in-form the self. "Down the hill fell Jack and Jill / And you came tumbling after / 'Cause of original sin" reads the second verse of "What Would You Say." Matthews connects falling with sinning, as well as with death: "A lifetime's passed you by" and "Everyone goes in the End" are phrases repeated or echoed throughout the song, which finally proceeds to a cryptic reference to memory: "Every dog has its day every day has its way / Of being forgotten—'Mom, it's my birthday.'"

"What Would You Say" is followed by "Satellite." Here Matthews again makes use of the rhymes of our youth, but with a twist. Instead of "Twinkle, twinkle little star" we get "Satellite in my eyes / Like a diamond in the sky / How I wonder. / Satellite strung from the moon / And the world your balloon / Peeping Tom for the mother station." A satellite provides a synoptic view. The image of a satellite also connotes circularity, the orbit of life, which goes 'round and 'round until we crash and are likely forgotten. A Christian history gives us a beginning and an end. In Matthews's universal history we are in perpetual motion, with no end save death. Call this Matthews's version of the idea of the eternal return of the same. Between life and death is but change for the worse: "Winter's cold spring erases / And the calm away by the storm is chasing / Everything good needs replacing."

But it is not nature's defects against which Matthews rails. It is nature's malleability at the hands of those with scientific prowess. Matthews seems to decry what the scientific Enlighteners celebrated. The song "Satellite" captures the tension between nature and technology. The song moves from a natural to a technological orb: "Satellite, headlines read / Someone's secrets you've seen / Eyes and cars have been / Satellite dish in my yard." The dish brings "Television," through which we merely "bounce 'round the world . . . five senses reeling." Matthews aptly follows this idea up with a song titled "Rhyme and Reason." (Note that it is not called "Rhyme *or* Reason.") The poet-singer-songwriter fails at resolving the tension between these two modes of knowing just as much as does the philosopher: "Oh well oh well so here we stand / But we stand for nothing." A few lines later the protagonist is as "good as dead." Dead may be "good," insofar as it silences the nagging voices of reason that speak against reason.

"My head aches—warped and tied up / I need to kill this pain." Madness is bliss. Ecstasies provide temporary relief from the anxiety of living. We fight reason with chaos. Yet Matthews remains a thinking man: "My head won't leave my head alone / And I don't believe it will / 'Til I'm dead and gone." He again evokes theological language to capture the conflicts of the self, for he "know[s] these voices must / Be my soul." Does Matthews really believe he has a conscience? A soul? Confusion compounded by confusion. "Oh man oh how I wish I didn't smoke / Or drink to reason with my head / But sometimes this thick confusion / Grows until I cannot bear it all / Needle to the vein." *Under the Table and Dreaming* is replete with contemplations that collapse or eradicate the distinction between thought and mania. Lines such as "Reason—my reason / Take my head off this terror," "Requesting some enlightenment / Could I have been anyone other than me?" and "hey reckless mind" speak to a union of mind and madness.

In the album *Crash,* Matthews continues to explore the dilemmas of a fragmented and disjointed life. In "So Much to Say" the singer-philosopher-poet claims that he needs no afterlife in order to experience hell: "I say hell is the closet I'm stuck inside / Can't see the light." Nor can we overcome or transcend this present hell by the expectation of Heaven, a concept that is derided by the album as a whole. Indeed, the Creator is to be mocked first and foremost, for he is to blame for the expectation itself, and hence for all of those things we strive for as if we were going to reach Heaven by, through, and with them: "And my Heaven is a nice house in the sky / Got central heating and I'm alright." Materialism and greed are the effects of a distorted and pernicious spiritual expectation—or the distortion of spirit by identifying it with matter. Secularism and materialism are the diseases of a soul that fails to understand what satisfies it: "I eat too much / I drink too much / I want too much," I am a "greedy little pig" ("Pig," *Before These Crowded Streets*).

There is a ray of hope, though, for we can turn our vices into virtues. For his part, Matthews turns his own lusty greed against God: "I told God, I'm coming to your country / I'm going to eat up your cities, / Your homes, you know / I've got a stomach full it's not / A chip on my shoulder / I've got this growl in my tummy / And I'm gonna stop it today." "Cry Freedom" is a beautiful ballad that offers a secular, humanistic prayer after we "Let this flag burn to dust / And a new a fair design be raised." However, greed stubbornly remains a vice even when it is turned against God, leaving Matthews haunted by a dilemma. "Hands and feet are all alike / But gold between divide us / Hands and feet are all alike / But fear between divide us." We are the instruments of our emancipation and hence of our own destruction. The crucifixion hovers in the background.

In "Proudest Monkey," Matthews gives us a story of origins that dispenses with God's. He meets our all-too-human maladies on natural rather than supernatural terms. We first jettison the biblical story of creation, or so it seems: "Swing in this tree / Oh I am bounce around so well / Branch to branch / limb to limb you see / All in a day's dream." Consider the importance of the dream as a state of being—in and out of consciousness, knowing and not knowing, seeing with eyes closed. While in the trees, "Like the other monkeys here / I am a humble monkey." We go back to the beginning and discover that we possess a natural innocence that makes for a simple and uncomplicated communion with our fellow simians. No original sin here. The scourge of pride is not yet visible, but we don't have to wait long. The thinking man is not only an ape; he is a being with reason and speech. Curious George "climbed out of these safe limbs / Ventured away." He stands erect. "Walking tall, head high up and singing." That he is still singing holds promise.

The solitary ape comes to dwell in crowded streets: "I went to the city / Car horns, corners and the gritty / Now I am the

proudest monkey you've ever seen / Monkey see, monkey do."
But the problem is not pride alone. Matthews speaks about the
mutation of pride into vanity and shame. The evil discovered
by the curious, wandering ape prompts the desire for a life that
is akin to life prior to the eating of the fruit from the Tree of
Knowing Good and Evil. But he is now "civilized"—and a
creature of reason no longer possesses the innocent bliss that
characterized the noble savage in Eden. He is literally reflective:
"Then comes the day / Staring at myself I turn to question me."
The civilized ape acquires an interior life, and nostalgia sets in:
"I wonder do I want the simple, simple life that I once lived in
well." It was "quiet then" and "in a way they were the better
days." But "now I am the proudest monkey you've ever seen."
Humility is no longer possible without the sting of humiliation.
The philosophically inclined will notice that these ruminations
read as if they were lifted from Jean-Jacques Rousseau's proto-
Darwinian *Second Discourse*.

Whereas "Proudest Monkey" describes our descent from
the tree, "Big Eyed Fish" (*Busted Stuff*) describes our emergence
from the sea, providing another perspective on evolution: "Look
at this big-eyed fish swimming in the sea / Oh how it dreams
to be a bird / Swoop and diving through the breeze." Just as
the monkey's descent proves morally fatal, so does the fish's
ascent: "So one day, caught a big old wave up on to the beach /
Now he's dead you see / Beneath the sea is where a fish should
be." Theological overtones abound. We lose life by seeking it.
Would the obverse be true? We cry out to God: "But oh God
/ Under the weight of life / Things seem brighter on the other
side." The problem, of course, is that there is no "other side,"
yet we remain possessed by the expectation: "You see this crazy

man decided not to breathe / He turned red and blue—purple, colorful indeed / No matter how his friends begged and pleaded / The man would not concede / And now he's dead you see / the silly man should know you got to breathe." Matthews then reminds us of the "Proudest Monkey," for the very next verse reads: "You see the little monkey sitting up in his monkey tree / One day decided to climb down and run off to the city / But look at him now lost and tired living in the street / As good as dead you see what a monkey does—stay up your tree." Whether our perspective is from on high or from below, we remain encased in an all-too-human life of contradiction and strife.

mothers and fathers

Matthews's meditations on beginnings bring us to mothers and fathers, feminine and masculine, gender and the engendered. The Oedipus complex provides a useful metaphor to capture this complicated whole. In *Remember Two Things,* the juxtaposition of nature's feminine and masculine modes serves numerous purposes. Is there really a feminine or nurturing side to nature, and if so, is Matthews drawing a comparison between masculine technological mastery over nature and feminine care? In "One Sweet World," which follows "Satellite" on *Remember Two Things,* we return to science: "Nine planets round the sun / Only one does the sun embrace / Upon this watered one / So much we take for granted." Gratitude, however, is childlike, and thus associated with the maternal: "So let us sleep outside tonight / Lay down in our mother's arms / For here we can rest safely." This feeling of gratitude is also ephemeral. "If green should turn to grey / Would our hearts still bloody be / And if the mountains crumble away / And the river dry / Would it stop the stepping feet." And if this is the case, then "Take all that we can get / When it's done / Nobody left to bury here / Nobody left to dig the holes / And here we can rest safely."

Matthews's feminine themes are, predictably, laced with erotic language. Consider the cryptic "Minarets." Minarets are tall spires atop Islamic mosques with projecting balconies from which a muezzin summons the faithful to prayer, so with this image Matthews goes both phallic and multicultural. We should also keep in mind that the jagged peaks in the Sierra Nevada Mountains of California are also referred to as "minarets." In any case, from the heights of minarets, Matthews tells us, "Santa Maria" chooses "your children." The "virgin child" is the prize of our "wars" that "all our time faith [is] justifying." The pristine feminine is violated. "Brother caged Babylon will fall / Sister chained and bound, beaten and bleeding." A brother—that is, our own flesh and blood—commits rape. The war in and for the soul, in other words, is a civil war. We are the victims of our own nature, an idea symbolized by the theme of reflection: "God has grown / Alone till a man looking glass in his hand / He is holding up to you." We respond: "What you see is human / Screaming from the minarets."

"Seek Up" follows. But instead of ascending, as in "Minarets," we now descend, a coupling reminiscent of that between "Proudest Monkey" and "Big Eyed Fish." We again reconsider our predicament by questioning the idea of our original goodness and the Father's care. "Sometimes I feel like I'm falling / Fall back again, fall back again." There is a disjunction between material and immaterial, internal and external. "Oh, life it seems a struggle between / What we think and what we see." Reason seems inextinguishable. For a believer, the civil war of the soul is pacified and subsequently overcome by salvation. "Seek Up" rejects this solution: "I'm not going to change my ways / Just to please you or appease you." We must struggle on our own, on nature's terms, not the divine's: "Inside a crowd, five billion proud / Willing to punch it out / Right, wrong, weak, strong." Here Matthews returns to a nursery rhyme: "Ashes to ashes all fall down / Look about around this round / About this merry-go-round around." No need to look up or down, since there is no verticality to our existence, no transcendence, but only around and around, for there is only the eternal recurrence of the same. (This same nursery rhyme reappears near the center of *Some Devil*'s "Gravedigger"—one of Matthews's biggest hits.) "Seek Up" asserts God's maliciousness: "If at all God's gaze upon us fall / His mischievous grin, look at him." Instead of remembering where we came from and what we supposedly are, let us forget. The solution to our internal conflict is to abandon, release, even surrender. "Forget about the reasons and / The treasons we are seeking / Forget about the notion that / Our emotions can be swept away / Forget about being guilty / We are innocent instead / For soon we will all find our lives swept away."

life as death

It is evident that the horizon of death haunts Matthews, and it thus deserves scrutiny. For Matthews is not simply speaking about the obvious, that we all die; death is Matthews's way of broaching the possibility of nothing. "Nothing" is important to us for several reasons. We believe that we are what we make of ourselves. "Deconstruction" is merely a fancy term for the view that we are by nature constructed beings and thus open to deconstruction as a way of finding out what we are. But if we repudiate nature as a permanent standard, and if we also repudiate God, this deconstructionist project is bound to wind up at nothing. Nothing is prior. God creates ex nihilo, or out of nothing. Would our annihilation, then, be a way to get back to the beginning, as it was for Christ? And what does an awareness of a primal nothing mean for our lives? If there is no eternal justice, no final reward or retribution, how should I then live? Or if I choose to suspend judgment on the entire matter, how do I live out my skepticism in a world of good and evil? Is the proper response to such ignorance faith?

Between no-thing and some-thing there is the self. If God created the material world, pride is akin to original sin because it is a feeling aroused by the misguided belief that we own, possess, and thus make ourselves. But if God made us, we did not make ourselves. We are not self-generating. We therefore do not own ourselves. That is why the Christian response to pride is charity, why eros is replaced by agape, possessive love by a love that is (supposedly) self-less, or truly humble. The Christian believes that we evacuate ourselves to find God's grace and love. We become no-thing before we are properly some-thing.

Compare this Christian understanding to, say, the Gnosticism of New-Age spiritualism, which invites us to surrender to the forces of nature or, therapeutically, to the pull and ministrations of the unconscious as a way of combating the tyrannical impulses of the self. Mystical eroticism promises complete self-abandonment in the service of self-possession. There are also existential responses to the void, both theistic (e.g., Kierkegaard) and atheistic (e.g., Nietzsche, Sartre, Camus). Can we actively pursue nothing? Suicide is one of Matthews's perennial themes. Contemplating this possibility reveals the power of will. We can affirm ourselves against the void in the name of freedom understood as nothing. From the power of the will to the Will to Power. Our current fascination with Eastern religions is intimately connected with this impetus to annihilate the self. We elevate nothing to the highest virtue under the name of freedom, secular or religious.

The darkness overwhelms Matthews just as do the light-promising alternatives. Returning to "Seek Up," we find our singer-protagonist contemplating all of life's injustices and inequities: "Sit awhile with TV's hungry child / Big Belly Swelled / Oh, for a price of a coke or a smoke / Keep alive those hungry eyes / Take a look at me, what you see in me / Mirror look at me / Face it all, face it all again." An enlightened world is too bright, too noisy. Reflection is painful. Too revealing. The truth has a numbing effect. We ate the fruit. And now "You seek up an emotion / And your cup is overflowing / You seek up an emotion / Sometimes your well is dry." Numb and null. But this is not the kind of nothing Matthews ultimately seeks, or can seek if he wants to affirm something true about himself and the universe. Instead, he finds mindless indulgence. Masochism and sadism.

Is there some power, some force in the darkness that I can call forth in an effort to free myself from the light and the perpetual and agonizing thoughts enlightenment brings? "Seek

Up" finds an answer that is for Matthews as enticing as it is dangerous: "You seek up a big monster / For him to fight your wars for you." But what is conjured up in the darkness is liable to devour the conjurer. Matthews finds hate everywhere because his perspective is constituted by hate. He is possessed by hate itself: "But when he finds his way to you, the devil's not / Going—ha ha." Matthews leaves us mid-sentence. He does not tell us what the Devil says. We merely hear his laughter. Matthews wants more. He demands: "Say, say." This line stands apart and alone. We then return to "my grave" in the next verse.

christmas

As if to soften the conclusion implied by the demonic suggestions of *Remember Two Things,* Matthews concludes with "Christmas Song." Now we come to Christ. That this song is on many people's Christmas mix CDs demonstrates Matthews's seductive power and influence, for it is anything but an affirmation of Christ. Perhaps we find ourselves in the kind of despair that demands religion, but when Matthews finds his way to Christ he does not find what a Christian finds. The song begins by portraying a union between man and woman, husband and wife: "She was his girl; he was her boyfriend / She be his wife; take him as her husband." Erotic imagery returns, as does the tension between male and female: "A surprise on the way, any day, any day." Before us is the nativity. After the three wise men shower the newborn with "love, love, love," Matthews, just as he does with nursery rhymes, takes some creative license with the biblical story: "Not very much of his childhood was known / Kept his mother Mary worried / Always out on his own / He met another Mary for a reasonable fee, less than / Reputable as known to be." Not much is known about the young Jesus, but Matthews freely speculates: Jesus is out whoring. Dan Brown would be pleased. Nothing less is expected of a man full of "Love love love / Love love is all around."

But abundant love is not to the Father's liking: "Jesus Christ was nailed to his tree," forsaken like the rest of us. Unlike Matthews, Jesus is confused by the intentions of the Father. "Said 'oh, Daddy-o I can see how it all soon will be / I came to shed a little light on this darkening scene / Instead I fear I've spilled the blood of my children all around.'" This reference is to bloodshed generally, but it is also to that redemptive bloodshed to which we are all invited: the Eucharist. "He said 'eat this bread and think of it as me / Drink this wine and dream it will be / The blood of our children all around / The blood of our children all around.'" Wine induces a dream, and the dream bloodshed. Matthews repeats it three times, as if he were Jesus's betrayer: "The blood of our children all around." Jesus then again questions himself and the work of his father. "Father up above, why in all this anger do you fill / Me up with love / Fill me love love love /Love love love /Love love / And the blood of our children all around."

Matthews presents us, then, with the betrayal of a tyrant father, intimations of a nurturing mother, conflict between an intense love and an intense hate, and an image of the confusing and contradictory inheritance codified in our nature and running through our veins. He wants to dramatize the struggle between what we know and what we are, between the desire to know and the desire to be. He perceives the serpentine character of knowledge, first sought and then spurned as the very source of our misery, and the inescapable tension between our desire to achieve technological mastery of chaos and our desire to surrender mindlessly to that same chaos. The weight of these issues presses against a sensitive, loving, and angry soul that yearns for beauty, communion with his fellow men and women, understanding, even transcendence.

Beginning with *Before These Crowded Streets,* virulence against the Father, his embodiment in Christ, and the possibility of taking recourse in the Devil in the battle against God take center stage in Matthews's lyrics. There is a climax of sorts here. Musically, *Before These Crowded Streets* is the darkest Matthews album, jazzy, folksy, with deep saxophones and heavy beats, above which we hear Matthews crying at the top of his voice with rage and desperation. Lyrically, the album is also the darkest and most seductive in his catalog. It doesn't necessarily start that way. The title of the first song, "Pantala Naga Pampa," is a loose translation of Tamil that means "I have a python in my pants," an expression supposedly often uttered by one of Matthews's Indian cooks. The song itself is but four lines and hardly threatening: "Come and relax now / Put your troubles down / No need to bear the weight of your worries / Yeah, let them all fall away." There is no conscious or conscientious link between the track's title and its lyrics. As the album develops, however, one wonders if the title is not meaningful indeed, functioning simultaneously as a warning of impending sexual danger and as a seductive invitation to yield.

Many of the themes developed in this chapter play themselves out in a song titled "Rapunzel," no doubt a reference to the story by the Brothers Grimm, a Faust- or Genesis-like tale of temptation, vanity, dangerous powers illicitly harnessed, forbidden plants, paid for by one's own offspring, adolescence and sexual flowering, virginity, innocence, and dangerous knowledge. Unlike the opening song, there is nothing subtle about the innuendo in "Rapunzel." "Open wide / Oh so good I'll eat you / Take me for a ride / In your sweet delicious / Perfect little mouth / Thereupon I linger / You will have no doubt / That I'll do my best for you, I do, love . . ." The association of sex with consumption adds an ominous quality to the craving. And Matthews links the song to the Last Supper. "I think the world of you / All of my heart I do / Blood through my veins for you / You alone have all of me / I give my world to you / To you I will be true." For the love of the world we give ourselves. Or we give what is most dear. God did it, why not me?

By way of the Christ Matthews arrives at eroticized violence. This is not too far removed from Friedrich Nietzsche's own celebration of Greek Dionysian orgies. But there is a difference. Unlike Nietzsche, before the abyss Matthews blinks. To borrow from another immoralist (Machiavelli), the crucifixion leaves Matthews both satisfied and stupefied. Satisfaction comes from the discovery of powers akin to God's that can then be turned against God. Let us make virtue out of vice. Stupefaction follows from the realization that those very powers are morally ambiguous, if not inherently evil. If we are beyond good and evil, say, like God himself, there is no morally unambiguous justification for slaying the demonic God by demonic means. Matthews's confusion is borne out in the remainder of the album.

Immediately following "Rapunzel," the song "Last Stop" mocks the person who believes "that you are the chosen one." The following line is either a vacillation or an extension of his contempt: "Oh no / Gracious even God / Bloodied on the cross / Your sins are washed enough." The singer sympathizes with the "mother's cry," which desperately wonders, "Is hate so deep / Must my baby's bones / This hungry fire feed?" Not just mothers suffer, though. The world itself is a "symphony of death." The protagonist is compelled to "scream." He knows that "right is wrong now." And yet the "chosen one" continues to speak. In desperation, Matthews screams, "Shut up you big lie / This black and white lie." He marshals his forces to combat the distinction between good and evil, to "break it down / So it's not so black and white." He also marshals his own righteous indignation to fight against righteous indignation. Screaming, "You're righteous, you're righteous . . . / You're always so right," he sees himself in what he hates, hates what he hates, and so in doing cannot simply hate hate. So he resorts to mockery: "There you are nailing a good tree." In other words, Matthews takes pity on the tree rather than the man. He even asks the crucified God to plead for forgiveness: "Then say forgive me, forgive me."

In "Spoon," the album's final track, Matthews takes this demand back—God does not deserve the opportunity. "Red blood sand / Could Dad be God? / Crosses cross hung out like a wet rag / Forgive you? / Why? / You hung me out to dry." Faithful to Nietzsche's spirit, he laughs: "Laughing out loud makes it all subside." And in "Don't Drink the Water" he contemplates a final or conclusive silence: "What's that you say / Your father's spirit still lives in this place / Well, I will silence you." That silence is sealed with the death of God: "What's this you say / You feel a right to remain? / Then stay and I will bury you." Indeed, "Dreamed I Killed God" is the title of a song Matthews chose not to release but is widely circulated among fans.

Matthews's journey into the depths of his soul renders suspect or at least paradoxical any attempt to establish good and evil on a secure footing. Matthews seeks good and in the process finds it necessary to embrace evil, which he justifies by pointing to God's evil. We live, as Matthews is at pains to point out, with anger, love, a sense of justice and injustice, hatred, compassion, fear, and hope. We even project these feelings beyond ourselves and beyond this life. Matthews takes a journey to hell in the hopes of discovering and harnessing the psychological powers needed to banish the psychological terror that flows from the demonic God. This, however, is not a justification Matthews can accept wholeheartedly, for it makes him into the very thing he hates. And so he courts nothingness. But can we be silent? Can we be still? For an active being who wants to be of consequence in the world, silence and inactivity are alternatives hard to square with intense love and hate. Matthews wants to establish his own space in the world in order to assert himself for all to see. Indifference is not the solution. Is war? There is a part of Matthews that loathes war. He wars against war, not least our present war. We thus find Matthews's retreat to silence tenuous and short-lived.

"The Space Between" (*Everyday*) is a case in point. Here, we should think of space in astronomical terms as well as in human terms, that is, as the space we occupy and as the space that separates us from what is not us. It is the place of or for retreat and thus for individuation. I need to discover me, and this means discovering that I am not you. One has to wonder if this quest is not simultaneously the source of Matthews's alienation, for he cannot bear the individuality he seeks. The alienation of the so-called "in-dividual" (the un-divided self) is twofold: between a common, shared humanity and me; and between the natural or created universe and me. The opening verse of "The Space Between" says that "You cannot quit me so quickly / Is no hope in you for me / No corner you could squeeze me / But I got all the time for you, love / The space between / The tears we cry is the laughter that keeps us coming back for more / The space between / The wicked lies we tell and hope to keep safe from the pain." We want to be individuals, distinct and diverse, and yet we also want to feel as though we are part of the world, as though we are an essential part of someone else.

How do we express this tension or paradox? Words are deceptive: "Will I hold you again? / These fickle, fuddled words confuse me / Like 'Will it rain today?' / We waste the hours with talking, talking / These twisted games we're playing." Sex? But that too subsides. Lost, we end up in the Devil's embrace: "Look at us spinning out in the madness of a rollercoaster / You know you went off like the devil in the church / In the middle of a crowded room / All we can do, my love / Is hope we don't take this ship down." The Devil is in the church. In "What You Are" we learn that "Hoping to God on high / Is like clinging to straws / While drowning, oh." But look at what we cling to now: "What you are / Is the beast in the lover's arms / What you are / Is the devil in the sweet, sweet kiss / What you are / Is missing a piece / What you are / Is a puzzle to me." Like Coldplay, Matthews is caught "Twisted between time and dreams," being in time and thinking himself out of time, a "place so full of color yet overflowing / Always in black and white." Dreams allow us to be out of time, or to be not fully conscious in time. But language confuses and makes choice difficult. "All this talk about / Endless words without / Nothing's done." Choose we must. Limbo is no space to live. But then Matthews does not want an either/or. He reaches out to a comprehensive nothing. "There's no God above / And no hell below / Oh, it's here with us / It's up to us / To keep afloat."

Busted Stuff poignantly captures the vacillation, confusion, the paralysis engendered by the failure to discriminate, the mindless and passionate eruption borne of existential dread and ennui. "Grey Street" sings of the conflation of black and white, good and evil. Here the quest ends up in grey, and we find Matthews numb and null yet again. "I live on the corner of Grey Street and the end of the world." The Last Man has no Superman to lift him. In "Where Are You Going" Matthews admits, "I am no superman / I have no answers for you / I am no hero, ah that's for sure." Some hope emerges in "You Never Know." We are "Sitting still as stone watching, watching." And a sense of justice will not allow the idea of God to vanish altogether: "What if God shuffled by?" The inertia brought about by indulgence in extremes brings reason back into view: "One day we might see / Doing not a thing / Breathing just to breathe / We might find some reason." If not reason, then some god: "Lying on the roof, counting / The suns that fill the sky, I wonder if / Someone in the heavens looking back down on me, I'll never know / So much space to believe." A light flickers: "It won't be so long now / Out of the darkness comes light like a flash." But like all else in the Matthews universe it does not amount to much. Every day "should be a good day to die."

some devil

We find ourselves back to Christ after the journey from Christ. Engulfed by an existential quagmire, our singer-protagonist wonders, "What would Jesus do?" According to Matthews, "He'd shake his head like an angry mother." It seems that if Jesus were brought to his senses he too would recognize the evil work of the Father. There is no way out of loving what we hate and hating what we love. Instead of being stuck in reverse or going forward and backward, Matthews travels in circles: "Begin to ending is really just a go round and round and round / And as I stand here—the ground beneath is nothing more than one point of view." The next song is titled "Grace is Gone." From there we proceed to "Digging a Ditch," and the album concludes with "Bartender" (Matthews's former occupation). From the sovereign bartender in the sky, the singer-protagonist orders the "wine you gave Jesus / That set him free, after three days in the ground." The prospects for resurrection drive him to prayer: "I'm on bended knee I pray / Bartender please." But the holy wine does not atone: "Bartender you see, the wine that's drinking me / Came from the vine that strung Judas from the devil's tree / His roots deep, deep in the ground."

Some Devil extinguishes the lingering hopes for meaning and salvation that emerge in *Busted Stuff*. That requires one final reconciliation with the Devil. The album opens with a song devoted to a creature now extinct. It is also a world in which "Fears would arise / That if you went too far, you'd fall." In such a world, "Why would you play by the rules?" There is prayer in "Trouble": "Pray your mercy shine on me / Pray your mercy shine." But in "Save Me," Matthews ends up mocking this very hope. As we should expect by now, a biblical story is evoked only to be transformed: "I'm driving through the desert I met a man / Who told me of his crazy plan / He'd been walking there for twenty days / He was going to walk on / For twenty more." The Devil is the singer-protagonist himself. He tempts Jesus. "Said 'How about a drink or a bite to eat?'" Jesus responds by saying, "No, my faith is all I need." Matthews dwells on that statement and then taunts Jesus: save me "if you can." We cannot live without belief, even if this means belief in nothing. "You don't need to prove a thing to me / Just give me faith, make me believe." Matthews wonders: "am I too far gone"? Jesus cannot deliver faith. Miracles prove nothing. "I don't need you to stall for some time, no / I don't need you to turn water into wine, no / I don't need you to, to fly / I'm just asking you to save me." Then the chorus taunts Jesus: "Might try saving yourself." We hear this in the background intermittently. In between, the singer-protagonist says he is "gonna save" himself. There are also sexual overtones to the encounter. Saving himself, Matthews delivers an oath: "I swear those lips shine . . . As it, the moon, the moon it shines." But since Matthews believes in Nothing, such an oath is, literally, incredible.

Strictly speaking, Matthews is a lunatic. We live by a partial light that does not allow us to discern the true nature of things, including ourselves. Here too we are lost. There is no coherent self to call our own, only the confused amalgamation of incompatible parts. Matthews might suggest that we travel without a compass, in a fluid and turbulent cosmic ocean, or perhaps upon Darwin's ponds.

Alpha and Omega

"Adam, there are those other new words die,
and death. What do they mean?"
"I have no idea"
"Well, then, what do you think they mean?"
"My child, cannot you see that it is impossible for
me to make even a plausible guess concerning a
matter about which I am absolutely ignorant? A
person can't think, when he has no material to
think with. Isn't that true?"
"Yes—I know it; but how vexatious it is. Just because I can't know, I all the more want to know."
— Mark Twain, "Autobiography of Eve"

Among the artifacts examined in this book none seems more deserving of contempt and righteous indignation than the novel *Fight Club,* by Chuck Palahniuk, and its film version, directed by David Fincher. After watching the movie, Roger Ebert summed up the sentiments of many of

those concerned with the decay of moral values and our pre-
cipitous descent into sexual license and violence: "*Fight Club*
is the most frankly and cheerfully fascist big-star movie since
Death Wish, a celebration of violence in which the heroes write
themselves a license to drink, smoke, screw and beat one another up." It is "macho porn—the sex movie Hollywood has
been moving toward for years, in which eroticism between the
sexes is replaced by all-guy locker-room fights." Regarding one
of the main protagonists (played by Brad Pitt), Ebert asks: "Is
Tyler Durden in fact a leader of men with a useful philosophy?" Durden's philosophy is succinctly captured in the claim
that "it's only after we've lost everything that we're free to do
anything," which, according to Ebert, sounds "like a man who
tripped over the Nietzsche display on his way to the coffee
bar in Borders. In my opinion, he has no useful truths. He's a
bully—Werner Erhard plus S&M, a leather club operator without the décor." Ultimately, "None of the Fight Club members
grows stronger or freer because of their membership; they're
reduced to pathetic cultists. Issue them black shirts and sign
them up as skinheads."

It is not the plot alone against which Ebert rails. The *Chicago
Sun-Times* critic protests against the "numbing effects of movies
like this," which "cause people [to go] a little crazy." A wave of
school shootings and a proliferation of fight clubs in the wake
of the movie lend credence to Ebert's concerns. And to aca-
demic critics such as myself he warns: "Although sophisticates
will be able to rationalize the movie as an argument against
the behavior it shows, my guess is that [the] audience will like
the behavior but not the argument. Certainly they'll buy tickets
because they can see Pitt and [Edward] Norton [another main

protagonist] pounding on each other; a lot more people will leave this movie and get in fights than will leave it discussing Tyler Durden's moral philosophy. The images in movies like this argue for themselves, and it takes a lot of narration to argue against them." Ebert concludes his review as unequivocally as he began. "*Fight Club* is a thrill ride masquerading as philosophy—the kind of ride where some people puke and others can't wait to get on again."

Responses such as Ebert's, however, seem to have had little effect on the growing popularity of *Fight Club*, a fact discernible to anyone who spends but a few minutes on the Web. And, just as Ebert predicted, both the book and the movie have attracted the fascination of academics, who now teach *Fight Club* in courses across the country. *Fight Club*'s brand of eroticized violence fits neatly with the various themes of liberation popular among today's professoriate, who believe eroticized violence is the sure path to enlightenment. To rebel against convention, or to deconstruct it, is to know.

What is it about Palahniuk's novel and Fincher's movie version that resonates in the souls of so many? If indignation is the right response to the movie and book, as Ebert and others claim it is, our indignation ought at least to be informed by our understanding. For *Fight Club* has exerted enormous appeal precisely because it is not the simple-minded work that Ebert and others think it is. These (both the book and the movie) are not stories about "boys being boys," yet another episode in Hollywood's misogynistic history. The protagonists in *Fight Club* are not reducible to a band of malcontents, whose depravity and remoteness from the mainstream concerns us only to the extent that their message translates into acts of violence. *Fight*

Club is a challenging tale about the end of time and the human yearning for rebirth.

Let us return to the Enlightenment. The philosophic proponents of our liberal modernity advanced a variety of teachings intended to tame the transcendent aspirations of the soul, or at least to make them compatible with wealth and the satisfaction of basic pleasures and needs—in short, compatible with what Thomas Hobbes called "commodious living." This is not a project devoid of strong arguments in its favor, the creation of modern liberty chief among them. But, as Palahniuk shows, there are good reasons to question the objectives of the modern, liberal, commercial experiment. However, Palahniuk's critique of (what several thinkers of the sixteenth and seventeenth centuries called) "commercial republicanism" is, in my estimation, something of a ruse. The ills of commercial life are only one part of a massive genetic defect we in the West inherit. This inheritance finds its source in the biblical God, Palahniuk's "the Great and Powerful . . . God and father."

In rethinking the Christian God, Palahniuk—like the other artists we have considered in this book—attempts to take us beyond good and evil. Ebert is correct to discern that Palahniuk is a nihilist. Even so, there are many good reasons for us to engage the meaning of nihilism, especially the kind of nihilism peddled by those such as Palahniuk. The question here, yet again, is this: what is in the Void?

In attempting to answer this question, we ought to pay special attention to the manner in which Palahniuk links nihilism to religion. His book plays on religion's call to nothing—that is, to a kind of death, for which there is a corresponding rebirth and resurrection. His apparent impiety comes to us in the shape of pious hopes and possibilities. How do we draw the distinction between pious and impious surrender? Is Palahniuk's work another iteration in that long history of nihilism which invites us to recognize the eternal recurrence of the same, a history without direction or end, without a narcotic providence or progress? Are we supposed to shed our pious illusions in order to embrace a dark god of chaotic urgings, whom we simultaneously acknowledge and conceal in various acts of self-creation, self-forgetting, and willful affirmation? Or does Palahniuk return us to a different kind of Nothing, to a new Genesis, from which Light, Word, and Life emerge? These are some of the questions that will animate our journey, during which I will focus on the book and not the film. Words reveal much more than a film ever can. And Palahniuk is a masterful ironist.

life as death

A brief synopsis. *Fight Club* is a story told from the perspective of a nameless narrator, who in the movie we know as "Jack." The narrator makes a living as a "recall campaign coordinator" (31). He determines whether car accidents are due to manufacturer failures, and, if so, whether to initiate a recall, a decision he must make according to the sole criterion of the car manufacturer's bottom line. Jack submits to his task, but at the expense of vigor, or spiritedness. He looks like a man without a soul living in a soulless, commercial regime. He gets some satisfaction combing through IKEA catalogs, furnishing his apartment on the consumer model of perfection. But as therapy, this is an imperfect solution.

A conscience stirs. Jack cannot sleep. Unable to find relief in medicine (his doctor refuses to prescribe sleeping medications), he seeks refuge in various support groups, which have been organized to help terminally ill patients cope with death. Our narrator is not terminally ill, but for some reason he finds comfort there. At the end of each session, members give each other the requisite hugs. In these moments Jack finds a momentary respite. He cries. And when Jack cries, he sleeps. His solution dissolves, however, when he discovers another "faker," named Marla Singer, attending the same group sessions. When Marla is present, our narrator's lie is exposed, principally to himself. He cannot cry, and he therefore cannot sleep.

At this point, Jack turns to Tyler Durden, whom he meets on an airplane during one of his endless business trips. Tyler helps the narrator see the banality of his life. Enticing and seductive, Tyler is spiritedness incarnate. Together, he and Jack found Fight Club, which allows our narrator to invigorate himself through cathartic violence. After each fight the narrator sleeps. Fight Club grows. Gradually, Jack sheds his worldly, consumer ways and is absorbed into Fight Club, which eventually morphs into "Project Mayhem," a band of "space monkeys" devoted to the "complete and right-away destruction of civilization" (125).

Let us turn to the narrative. The book opens with the narrator, who, we are told, is indebted to Tyler for his waiter's job. The debt to Tyler is juxtaposed against the narrator's vulnerability and fear. As we will shortly discover, the opening is also the end. The book begins with the concluding scene. Tyler "is pushing a gun in my mouth" (11), saying meanwhile that "the first step to eternal life is you have to die" (11). We do not hear

Tyler utter these words, however. We hear them from the narrator, Jack. What Tyler promises in his own words is that "'We really won't die'" (11). We are invited to juxtapose the original words we no longer hear as words, that eternal life is promised only with and after death, with the words we hear, that there is no death. The two statements are not identical, but neither are they incompatible or contradictory. One asks that we live by a horizon of "death," the other by a horizon absent of "death." Yet both seem to promise eternal life. That we confuse these utterances of the soul is understandable. Palahniuk opens his Destruction/Creation story with the great contest between Good and Evil, the Divine and Demonic. At the book's genesis Jack also tells us that "Tyler and I were best friends" (11). That is, Tyler and the narrator were once a unity whose relation is now in question.

Tyler goes on to explain in his own words why "this isn't really death" (11). To die is not to die. The Serpent is now visible. To heed Tyler's words will give us eternal fame, eternal youth. "We'll be legend. We won't grow old" (11). Tyler promises eternal life in this world, eternal memory founded on vanity. The promise of eternal youth appeals to our narcissism. Whether this "eternity" is a viable alternative to the other "eternity" remains an unanswered question, to this point. At this junction, Palahniuk chooses instead to provide a clue that might unravel the character and content of Tyler's promise. In what falls between audible speech and thought (he is speaking with a gun in his mouth), Jack says, "Tyler, you're thinking of vampires" (12). Tyler lives by night: "Because of his nature, Tyler could only work night jobs" (25). He is the Prince of Darkness. This may be life, eternal life, but at the expense of the narrator, and perhaps everything else that is not Tyler. At the end, which is also our beginning, all of this is visible to the narrator.

Here, in the scene which comes at the beginning of the book but at the end of the story, Tyler and Jack are standing on "top of the Parker-Morris building" (12). The building is about to explode, rigged to do so by Tyler. (For something that is about to go up in smoke, the building is aptly named.) We are told that the Parker-Morris building is the "world's tallest" (12), and so, symbolically at least, Tyler and Jack are on top of the world. But is this their rightful place. We learn that the wind is always cold there. And this "high up, the feeling you get is that you're one of those space monkeys. You do the little job you're trained to do. Pull a lever. Push a button" (12). From on high the "street below is mottled with a shag carpet of people, standing, looking up" (12). From Tyler and Jack's current perspective, all individuation is lost. Is this a privileged position? Would it be possible to see and feel differently if the vantage point were some other?

By taking us to the top of the world (cf. Matt. 4:1–11; Luke 4:1–13), Palahniuk revisits the theme of wholeness announced in the opening scene, but by different means and to different ends. On top of the world, the whole is coincident with our synoptic vision. While on top of the Parker-Morris building, the protagonists reflect on history, that is, the whole of human experience. Our present ills are only intelligible in light of what came before us. "Somewhere in the one hundred and ninety-one floors under us," Palahniuk writes, "the space monkeys in the Mischief Committee of Project Mayhem are running wild, destroying every scrap of history" (12). We are here to look at memory. Indeed, we later learn that the Parker-Morris building is not even Tyler's "real target." The exploding building is designed to collapse on the "national museum" (14).

Erasure and forgetfulness, memory and responsibility. I cannot be an autonomous being as long as I have obligations to bear. The past prevents us from living in the present. Forgetfulness and happiness go hand in hand. Charlie Kaufman's *Eternal Sunshine of the Spotless Mind* deals with the same theme. Having to bear the weight of the past is at odds with autonomy. The claim that Project Mayhem is out to destroy "every scrap of history" is immediately followed by a most curious statement about love, life, and death: "That old saying, how you always kill the one you love, well, look, it works both ways" (13). This saying does not come from Tyler's mouth, or even from the narrator, "Jack." It comes to us merely as "That old saying." Who is this person the narrator must kill (for the sake of love?), and who in turn wants to kill him? How is this person connected to some old or ancient memory and/or practice? How does this murder put the fragmented self together, or somehow ameliorate the present threat? In short, what is the "real" target? The crucified God is near.

Ironies abound. In order to identify what to destroy we must first remember. *Fight Club* is as much about remembering as it is about forgetting. We are the past and must therefore usher the past back in order to annihilate the past. That Palahniuk's novel begins at the end means that it is itself a remembrance, in the midst of which the narrator is remembering. The narrator recalls his association with Tyler, how Tyler and he were once friends, and the reasons he is now held hostage. Children of God are also children of Satan. At this point the narrator thinks of the murder he must commit. Let me suggest that the ancient memory Jack revisits includes (but is not wholly) Tyler himself. The quest for psychic wholeness has everything to do with our capacity to harness, tame, or in some way accommodate the Serpent—if we can. The "Crisis of Civilization" is, as Tom Wolfe suggests, a crisis of the soul. Those familiar with the film will recall the pyrotechnics at the conclusion, as civilization implodes. We marvel at the explosions, ignoring where they are actually taking place. "Project Mayhem" is literally a project, a projectile, and a projection. Tyler earns his living as a movie theater "projectionist" (27). So, is modernity a project?

On the heels of the "old saying," the narrator describes in intimate detail how the Parker-Morris building will explode, glass spraying, desks flying out the windows. He also takes the reader through a countdown, beginning at ten minutes. We are lost in number. We are also soon lost in the details of bomb building—"[t]he three ways to make napalm" (13) and the like. Sufficiently distracted, we "just totally forget about Tyler's whole murder-suicide thing while we watch another file cabinet slip out the side of the building and the drawers roll open midair, reams of white paper caught in the updraft and carried off on the wind" (13). Here is an example of Palahniuk at his ironic best, quietly telling the reader that at the heart of this novel is Tyler's "whole murder-suicide thing." The sovereign issue has been deflected, we might say, and that deflection draws our attention to the bombs, violence, and all those attractions that make for good movies. But it is possible to see beyond the debris.

A writer as careful as Palahniuk demands that we take up this revelation in the context of the narrative. That Palahniuk's

first chapter is both the beginning and the end compels us to
wonder whether the psychological struggle identified here is
(at?) the beginning and/or the end, and how. Is the struggle
between competing voices and inclinations the original chaos
itself, out of which we create order? The Void? Nothing? Or
is the chaos the *end*, the point to which our current civilization brings us? Neither? Both? Is this chaos, then, omnipresent?
If so, is Palahniuk presenting us with a nominalist God, who
we must either embrace or against which we must muster our
various resources? To reduce these questions so as to make our
examination poignant: is the Void an ever-present possibility?
Yes. We die. And civilizations perish, and we have no reason
to think that America is exempt from the fate that awaits us
all individually and collectively. Is the perpetual cycle of decay
an indication that our so-called foundations are themselves genetically defective? Palahniuk's remarkable illumination of this
possibility poses the greatest challenge to readers and interpret-
ers. You may wish to return to the introduction.

If the incredulous reader thinks we have strayed too far,
consider what transpires as we move through the first chapter
of *Fight Club*. As the building is about to explode, the narrator
continues to rethink his friendship with Tyler. He ponders the
nature of the Beast he once befriended, or simply recognized
in himself. The narrator's thoughts are now clearly tinged with
regret. In our abysmal state, beyond good and evil, there is this
nagging thing we call guilt. What does this point to—an essence of some kind, or a cultural fabrication? But can one sever
the kinship between good and evil, without severing oneself?
We are at first tempted by a hopeful solution. Tyler tells the
narrator, "This is our world, now, our world . . . and those an-

cient people are dead" (14). To which the narrator offers this response: "If I knew how this would all turn out, I'd be more than happy to be dead and in Heaven right now" (14).

The promise of eternal life emerges in the context of a meditation about original sin. While on "top of the Parker-Morris building" with "Tyler's gun in my mouth," while "desks and filing cabinets and computers meteor down on the crowd around the building and smoke funnels up from the broken windows," the narrator comes to "know" this: "the gun, the anarchy, the explosion is really about Marla Singer" (14). The struggle in the soul between good and evil now turns into a struggle with and for a woman, with and for a certain type of man. "We have a sort of triangle thing going here. I want Tyler. Tyler wants Marla. Marla wants me" (14). We might have anticipated that a retelling of creation and Fall could not proceed without Woman. "So, Marla, how do you like them apples?" (37). This marvel (literally a mirror or wonder, akin to Prospero's Miranda) brings us face-to-face with perennial themes that are always implicated with creation and Fall, among them, the relationship between knowledge and death, knowledge and life, desire, wisdom, lust, sex, marriage, obedience, loyalty, and punishment, all bound in some way to love. As strange as this may sound, *Fight Club* is a book about *eros*—perhaps about the possibility of *agape*: "I don't want Marla, and Tyler doesn't want me around, not anymore. This isn't about love as in caring. This is about property as in ownership" (14). The introduction of Marla compels us to rethink the ordering of the soul, but now in terms of Palahniuk's tripartite division. The relationship among the parts is complicated by the fact that "[w]ithout Marla, Tyler would have nothing" (14). Bear in mind that the issue here is not simply who possesses whom, though surely that is a part of the problem. In the context of the soul's fragmentation, the issue here is self-possession. In other words, who or what governs? Love? But is there love without possession? Is there charity? If Tyler is the narrator's projection, we have reason to believe that Marla is, too.

The narrator's confusions multiply now that he understands the peculiar dynamic of his soul, the contest between himself, Tyler, and Marla. But the introduction of Marla also promises enlightenment. Eve delights at the prospect of wisdom. Enter Sophia. Original sin now squarely in view, Palahniuk turns to the Christian solution. "Where would Jesus be if no one had written the gospels?" The narrator contemplates his worldly existence in a new light, the "light of the world." The quest for wholeness requires more than a flight from this world into "Heaven." "Thy Kingdom come, Thy will be done, On earth as it is in Heaven" (Matt. 6:10). The quest for wholeness may call for a synthesis between the claims of Heaven and the claims of earth. The narrator is now emboldened. "I tongue the gun barrel into my cheek and say, you want to be a legend, Tyler, man, I'll make you a legend. I've been here from the beginning. I remember everything" (14). Complete forgetfulness meets complete remembrance, darkness meets light, matter spirit, nothing everything.

to the trinity

Palahniuk opens his book by situating the reader in the midst of the great human struggle between good and evil, creation

and Fall. That struggle is at once psychic and physical, teleo-
logical and historical; it simultaneously involves the individual and civilization as a whole. If we are prepared to ascribe
a "crisis" to contemporary civilization, it is only properly understood in terms of the conditions, problems, and possibilities of the soul. And this means *understanding* the soul. Within
the soul we find Tyler Durden. He is the perfect anti-thesis,
complete darkness, complete forgetfulness. He is Nothing.
And he has a gun in our mouths. Tyler is always there, and I
won't say merely lurking in the subconscious. Tyler is loved.
Eros and spiritedness are linked. He is the kind of person
one is inclined to befriend. He is more than a neighbor and
demands more than charity. Tyler the Beast seems to have a
claim on us.

We are inclined to take flight to whatever it is that is not
Tyler. We look to "Heaven," first, as the alternative. "Everything"—that is, completeness and happiness—depends on our
capacity to evacuate ourselves, from ourselves, to seek nothing: "Evacuate. Now. Soul clear of body" (36–37). But if this
is true, the struggle between good and evil seems to turn on the
prospects of competing nothings. Lest we forget, at the heart of
Palahniuk's book is Tyler's "murder-suicide thing." The narrator is holding a gun in his own mouth. Who do we trust? We
are at an impasse. It is at this point in the narration that woman enters. Why she enters, what she represents, and how she
seems to save the narrator from "death" are questions we must
now examine fully. It is true that understanding the "murder-
suicide thing" is the sovereign issue of the novel. But, following
Palahniuk's cue and clue, the key to unlocking the "whole murder-suicide thing" lies in the mystery of Marla. It is here that

matters get considerably darker. Our search for light requires that we turn to the novel's second chapter.

Our reading of the first chapter implied that the voices in our narrator's head seem to come from a single source. The narrator says that Tyler says one must die in order to gain eternal life. Tyler responds in his own words by saying that to die is not to die. To "die" is rather to earn eternal and earthly fame. We deferred grappling with the origin of these voices in order to hear them distinctly. Palahniuk the author wants the ancient contest between good and evil to be present for the reader as well. Having heard the tormenting voices, it is now necessary to consider what it means for them to come from one source. Palahniuk's genesis takes us one step back, to that moment when chaos reigned and there was no light, to the unconscious, to the most primal, to what is beyond good and evil. Nothing.

The possibility that "God the Father" is the source of the apparently distinct voices passes by imperceptibly until we near the conclusion of the book. We are told that the narrator eventually comes to the conclusion that Tyler Durden is "the Great and Powerful . . . God and father" (199). We should recall that our beginning is also the end. What we learn at the end of the book is part of and thus sheds light on the beginning. That "God the Father" is himself beyond good and evil, or the source of good and evil, is not inconsistent with some readings of Genesis. On one plausible reading, the Serpent is an indispensable part of God's plan. The Fall is therefore predestined. God tempts his children, banishes them from the Garden, and then promises a return to bliss for their complete devotion and faith. "Tyler said if I loved him, I'd trust him" (89). In this interpretation, God is simultaneously Creator, Benefactor, Judge, Executioner, and Redeemer.

But if this is the original image of "Father," one cannot but question his goodness. Accordingly, our own guilt for an original transgression, as well as our faith in redemption, are also questionable. In fact, these are precisely the questions Palahniuk places in front of the reader in the guise of the narrator's own reassessment of his situation at the end of chapter 1. Hints about the character of the divine are scattered throughout the novel, especially in the discussions of fatherhood. In one such instance, Palahniuk writes: "If you're male and you're Christian and living in America, your father is your model for God. And if you never know your father, if your father bails out or dies or is never at home, what do you believe about God?" (141). There is no doubt Palahniuk takes a hard look at fathers. However, to read such remarks merely as a chastisement of deadbeat dads is to miss the forest for the trees. Palahniuk's meditation at the beginning and throughout the novel is squarely on the Father of all fathers, God himself. It is God as "Father" who decisively fails us. Or worse. "What you have to consider . . . is the possibility that God doesn't like you. Could be, God hates us" (141). "Father" is supposed to care. But he does not. This is not mere indifference. Seeing "Father" in this light may lead his children to wonder if their hopes for salvation, redemption, or "Heaven" are misplaced. We might have to banish guilt as well. In the midst of this narrative about fathers, Tyler seems to offer the narrator a different choice: "Which is worse, hell or nothing?" (141).

In the second chapter, Palahniuk develops the image of the chimerical God by juxtaposing his implicit suggestions about "God the Father" with some elaborate and less implicit suggestions about "God the Mother." Here, Palahniuk plays heavily on the relation between "femininity" and "care" (whether fairly or unfairly, the reader must decide). We learn in this chapter that the narrator meets Marla in the basement of the "Trinity Episcopal" church (17), during a support-group meeting for men with testicular cancer called "Remaining Men Together" (18). She is the only woman attending. The insomniac meets "woman" while searching for a release from his painful "reality." He looks for compassion, care, or some semblance of these amidst a group of denatured men. In, literally, the heart of God—that is, in the Trinity   the narrator discovers a woman surrounded by emasculated, sexless, and impotent men. To be blunt, woman is in the house or heart of God amidst (or perhaps sheltered or hidden by) priests. The narrator goes in search of religion to help him cope with living. He finds a "woman" within something that is strangely "womanly."

Among emasculated men and a questionable woman, the narrator meets Bob. They embrace. "BOB'S BIG ARMS were closed around to hold me inside, and I was squeezed in the dark between Bob's new sweating tits that hang enormous, the way we think of God's as big" (16). In the Trinity the narrator meets a God-man without male anatomy, but with a female's anatomy. God appears as an emasculated male. Bob's shoulders are the narrator's new "horizon" (16). But then, an emasculated male is not a female. So what is the divine female that seems to emerge in the image of God before us? "Big Bob was a juicer, he said. All those salad days on Dianabol and then the racehorse steroid, Wistrol. His own gym, Big Bob owned a gym" (21). Yet another search for perfection comes at the price of happiness. Bob said that "[h]e'd been married three times" (21). "He was bankrupt. He had two grown kids who wouldn't return his calls" (22). Bob is impotent now. His initial strength, if we can call it that, was temporary, for show merely. "He'd done product endorsements, and had I seen him on television, ever? The whole how-to program about expanding your chest was practically his invention" (21). Bob now finds himself at "Remaining Men Together" because "six months ago, his testicles were removed. Then hormone support therapy. Bob has tits because his testosterone ration is too high. Raise the testosterone level too much, you body ups the estrogen to seek a balance . . . too much estrogen, and you get bitch tits" (17). When the narrator is in Bob's arms, Bob's "big wet face settles down on top of my head, and I am lost inside. This is when I'd cry. Crying is right at hand in the smothering dark, closed inside someone else . . ." (17). In Bob's embrace, the narrator figuratively returns to the womb, that is, to his origin.

The perverted masculine and feminine God is captured in the image of Bob but not less so in the image of Marla. In one of the most controversial lines in the book (omitted from the movie), Marla says (after having sex with Tyler) that "she wanted to have Tyler's abortion" (59). Marla longs to kill what is most intimately woman, that which is so significantly the creation of a woman. "What Marla loves, she says, is all the things that people love intensely and then dump an hour or a day after" (67). Bob, as we know, grows "bitch tits." Marla too is referred to as a "bitch" (24). As if matters were not sufficiently complicated, during an episode in which Tyler is making soap we are told that he cannot complete his project without Marla's help. A key ingredient is missing. Tyler asks Marla to fetch some lye (66). When making a product whose purpose is to cleanse us, but which can be turned into explosives, the woman is called to introduce the lie/lye.

Palahniuk has no sanitized image of either the masculine or the feminine to offer us. The view of God as parent, whether masculine and/or feminine, possesses no redeeming qualities that we would want to emulate or even admire as noble. The solution to a God that is now exposed for what it is cannot be the crucifixion. For this too is from God. Aside from the initial revulsion generated by the vision of God before us, what is it exactly about the crucifixion that earns contempt? We enter Dave Matthews's territory. Remember the "murder-suicide thing." What we are taught to call our Father's mercy comes to us by way of the greatest sacrifice, the sacrifice of his greatest love. This is, curiously, a self-sacrifice as well, at least insofar as we are prepared to accept that God the Father and God the Son are one and the same. If God the Creator planned the Fall, did he also plan salvation? This would make the Creator a destructive and self-destructive God. His children seem to partake of this quality, too. As Tyler says, "Maybe self-improvement isn't the answer. . . . Maybe self-destruction is the answer" (49). The psychology of love and hate, pleasure and pain runs deep here. We are children of a grand confusion of pain and pleasure, beings capable of painful pleasures and pleasurable pains. The Fight Club itself is a poignant image of this fundamental confusion of pain and pleasure. The protagonists seek pleasurable pain, pleasurable pains to release them from what have become painful pleasures. *Fight Club* the book is an attempt to take us back to that beginning, the beginning in which chaos, creation, destruction, love, and hate exist in peculiar relation to one another. *Fight Club* is an exploration of the primal unconscious of pain-pleasure.

to the eucharist

As bleak as the picture before us is, we are not ready to draw a final conclusion. As we press on we discover that chapter 2 is composed of two stories; it is a story within a story. And the innermost story unfolds not in the basement of the "Trinity," but in another church, the "First Eucharist" (19). We might say, then, that we are going into the Trinity itself in order to explore the mystery of transubstantiation, the making of the Word into Flesh. Palahniuk is not yet done with his meditation on the Christ-God.

The second story begins by telling us that "Remaining Men Together" was not our narrator's first visit to a support group. "I went to my first support group two years ago, after I'd gone to my doctor about my insomnia, again" (18). He hadn't slept for three weeks, the narrator says. And "[t]hree weeks without sleep . . . everything becomes an out-of-body experience" (19). Here begins the first play on "body." When the narrator describes his condition to his physician, the "doctor said, 'Insomnia is just the symptom of something larger. Find out what's actually wrong. Listen to your body'" (19). Our disembodied narrator is told to listen to his body in order to discover the "real" source of his pain, which apparently is not physical, not located in his "body." If it were, then the doctor could prescribe the appropriate medications to alter the condition of the body. A little "valerian root and . . . more exercise" might help (19). If the narrator wants to see real pain, he "should swing by First Eucharist on a Tuesday night. See the brain parasites. See the degenerative bone diseases. The organic brain dysfunctions. See the cancer patients getting by" (19).

It seems as if our narrator is the only male at First Eucharist. At least, the first names given, Alice and Brenda, are women's. The third name is androgynous, Dover. Unlike his later visits to "Remaining Men Together," the narrator is now surrounded by women, and these women are withering away (unlike Bob, who is growing). The focus at this support-group session at First Eucharist is the story of a woman. Her name is Chloe. Chloe tells the narrator that the worst thing about brain parasites is that "no one would have sex with her" (19). She cannot find another body. And Palahniuk makes explicit that she only wants a body: "Not intimacy, sex" (19). Chloe does not discriminate. She wants another body to satisfy her desires, and to heighten them. Chloe has "pornographic movies" and other paraphernalia. The narrator is not aroused, however. "Chloe looking the way she is, I am nothing. Not even nothing" (20). Nothing. When he entered the Trinity, the narrator was greeted by an emasculated male looking like a woman. Now he enters the Eucharist and finds withering women, and one woman in particular whose sole remaining desire focuses exclusively on the body: "Screwing passed the time" (20). The prospects of "nothing" and of "death" return. Not even cathartic sex is available to her.

Chloe then takes the narrator through guided meditation. The narrator will be taken to the "garden of serenity" (20). "We close our eyes. . . . Chloe talked us up the hill to the palace of seven doors. Inside the palace were the seven doors, the green door, the yellow door, the orange door, and Chloe talked us through opening each door, the blue door, the red door, the white door, and finding what was there" (20). Seven is God's perfect number. His creation is completed in six days, but another is needed for rest. Rest is completion. Rest is the end. We could say that guided meditation takes the narrator to the complete or perfect place. There the narrator finds enlightenment. "Eyes closed, we imagined our pain as a ball of white healing light floating around our feet and rising to our knees, our waist, our chest" (20). Guided meditation takes us to the "light" itself. There is an affinity between this process of self-discovery and the path taken by some Eastern religions. Is this sarcasm? "Our chakras opening. The heart chakra. The head chakra" (20). Chloe then takes the narrator and the audience into a "cave." Here we discover our "power animal." "Mine," says the narrator, "was a penguin" (20). We cast a gaze on the featherless biped and no doubt laugh. After all, "Laughter Is the Best Medicine" (58).

The Da Vinci Code

We have infinite trouble in solving man-made
mysteries, it is only when we set out to discover
the secret of God that our difficulties disappear.
— Mark Twain

I n the beginning was Dan Brown. Before the beginning was
Tori Amos. The 2005 best-seller *Tori Amos: piece by piece* (by
Tori Amos and Ann Powers) explains Amos's protracted
struggle to reinterpret Christianity by drawing upon the 1945
discoveries of ancient manuscripts at Nag Hammadi (known
as the Gnostic Gospels). "Whether you like it or not," writes
Amos, Dan Brown's *Da Vinci Code,* which draws from the same
ancient documents, "struck a chord with the masses, whereby
the public began to look up to the Magdalene, to open up to the
Magdalene as a Being, not just as a demeaned prostitute" (59).
According to Amos, Mary Magdalene is an "idea" that captures the mysteries of woman "and precede[s] the Magdalene
by many years" (63). These mysteries focus on the power of

the feminine—what Amos calls Wisdom and Consciousness, or Sophia and Achamoth—and embody, Amos argues, Jesus's true teachings, which were violently and viciously suppressed by the church fathers. Recovering the spirit of the Magdalene does not mean that we must repudiate the image of the other celebrated Mary, however. Traditional Christianity gives us a "false split" between the Virgin Mary and the Magdalene, claims Amos. Within the human psyche "they must be joined, not polarized. . . ." By force and by fraud the "Virgin Mary has been stripped of her sexuality but has retained her spirituality; the Magdalene has been stripped of her spirituality but has retained her sexuality." Amos's task is to marry the two Marys (63–64). "I've asked myself, Is there a way to reach an orgasm and keep your spirituality intact?" (94). Can we put body and soul together after it was torn asunder?

This fundamental split is accompanied by a host of others, Amos tells us. For example, there is the "segregation of heart from mind, actions from consequences, of man from woman, of power from imagination, and of passion from compassion" (58). Amos seeks a new incarnation to overcome these oppositions: "I remember lying underneath [an afghan made of wool] and squeezing my legs and pretending Jesus was there" (68). Here is Amos's Eucharist. The new incarnation, however, is not of the Christ alone. With the album *Boys for Pele* (Pele is the Hawaiian goddess of fire), Amos "really started to explore the Dark Prince archetype" (85). Amos says that she "needed to access the Dark Prince in myself, instead of pulling in men who had access to it" (85). She even sought the help of a shaman "who was reputed to know how to take you on a spiritual journey by uncovering things you were avoiding in your view of yourself" (85). Through the aid of the shaman, Amos

> had a sexual/spiritual experience with a creature named Lucifer. The word Lucifer is from Latin, meaning "light-bearer," also defined as the planet Venus in its appearance as the morning star. The other Being I had an experience with was called Davide. He seemed like a blond angel figure. Light and dark. So to me they represented Dionysus and Apollo [cf. Nietzsche's *Birth of Tragedy*]—that's the best way to put it. In my Being I was merging, and I remember him saying to me, "The seed is being planted, a really important seed. You will be pregnant, but with yourself, with a part of yourself. You need to give birth to a part of yourself that has been cut out." Circumcised, I think was their word. A part of my soul had been circumcised. And they really made love to my woman in a way that I had never, ever—I mean, you want to talk about being loved out of my own purgatory. . . . (88–89)

Thus did Amos find her "demon lover" (89).

For Amos, the personal and spiritual is the political. Inevitably, we "come back to the question *What is political? What is social?*" And this requires us to reconsider the questions, "*What is a powerful male, a powerful female? How are those roles abused?*" (95, Amos's emphases). If we go "after that core" we don't "have to worry about who is part of the peace movement, who is part of Earth First, who is part of Amnesty International. That will take care of itself" (95–96). When we go to the core we "automatically invite both [masculine and feminine, good and evil] to come in and be characters in this play." Recovering sacred prostitutes and demons will advance the political struggle against patriarchy by allowing us to "crawl inside [the] psyche" of the powerful and dismember them. Amos wants to be "right back there in that pituitary and crawl in like a snake" (96). Turn the other cheek, love your enemies—these ideas are not part of the new Gospel preached here. As long as there is domination, "we must have dominatrices to correct that imbalance." Perhaps as a cryptic reference to Larry Wachowski (one of the brothers responsible for the blockbuster *Matrix* trilogy), who abandoned his childhood sweetheart and wife Thea to hook up with the sadomasochistic dominatrix Karin Winslow (you can't make this stuff up!), Amos says: "You know, I'm told that certain old-school men in the music industry require dominatrices to rebalance them so they can be ruthless in their work and immune to the pain they are inflicting. They're doing their penance, these entertainment industry cheeses who then subjugate their artists" (97). Brother Silas, step aside. Opus Dei is but foreplay.

The psycho-political transformation Amos intends to effect is described in *piece by piece*. But this book is merely a useful preface to her project. Song is Amos's most powerful weapon. "The joining of the profane and the sacred, or the passionate and the compassionate, happens right there on the keyboard. It reconciles a bond severed a long time ago. There's so much shame around passion's innate hunger, which sometimes can be deemed profane, but music can access its reality: that which has been sacred but has been severed" (64–65). The profane is sacred, Amos tells us, and the sacred profane. We are, once again, in a world beyond good and evil, and her songs provide access to that world: "I created musical codes from a very young age, so I could recall what was really happening in my life. I had to know where the knowledge was, so I stored it all in the songs. I store everything in the songs, everything. I'm leaving you clues and I'm giving you a chance to go on a little hunt" (43). Let the hunt begin.

tales of a librarian

Amos's songs capture a spiritual journey that begins with *Little Earthquakes* (1992), passes through *To Venus and Back* (1999), and comes to fruition in her last three albums: *Scarlet's Walk* (2002), *Tales of a Librarian* (2003, though it is actually a thoughtful and clever compilation of previous songs), and *Beekeeper* (2005). Let us begin with *Tales of a Librarian*, for there Amos selects and orders her pre-2002 recordings, providing, for us, a convenient way to assess her voluminous ouevre. We will conclude with *Scarlet's Walk* and *Beekeeper*, the first a rumination on America's history, the second on the American cultural landscape.

The title *Tales of a Librarian* may be an ironic reference to Amos's first band, Y Kant Amos Read. (Her philosophical proclivities were demonstrated early on.) Amos parses *Tales* into various categories and then places a song under each. In keeping with her cryptic playfulness, the songs (and hence the categories) as arranged on the CD jacket are not the same as the songs as they are arranged on the CD. For example, the first song on the album is "Precious Things" and falls under the category "Collective Biography." The first song in the booklet is "Tear in Your Hand" and falls under "Cosmology (Philosophy of Nature)," which is a subset of "Metaphysics." What do we make of this difference? Does the order in which we listen to songs provide an experience different from the one we obtain by reading through the lyrics? The distinction seems to be between the personal and the cosmic. Let us first consider the latter.

As we saw in the introduction, Amos's music is self-consciously created in the same spirit as Neil Gaiman's fantasy works. Gaiman, in fact, figures prominently in "Tear in Your Hand" ("me and Neil'll be hangin' out with the DREAM KING," sings Amos), which is fitting, since both Amos and Gaimain offer meditations on the possibilities open to us after the death of the Christian God. In a book titled *Hanging Out with the Dream King: Conversations with Neil Gaiman* (2004), Amos contributes a chapter that contains a few revelatory words about the Amos-Gaiman cross-fertilization. And Gaiman returns the favor, or so it seems, in his book *Anansi Boys*. Read the opening paragraph.

After "Tear in the Hand" and its reference to Gaiman comes a track titled "God," which is included by Amos under the heading "Christianity and Christian Theory." Here the assault on God the Father begins: "God sometimes you just don't come through." Like Palahniuk, Amos believes that God's failure is linked to the usual failure of men and of fathers. But unlike Palahniuk, she believes that there is a redeemable woman lurking behind the male image. God needs "a woman to look after [him]."

God's failure is puzzling to Amos because the totality of experience speaks to both good and evil. Amos praises the Creator for the "pretty daisies." But how does a world of such beauty also include such horror? In search of answers, Amos interrogates God. She wants to know "what you've been doing about things here." Look at what takes place in the name of God: "a few witches burning gets a little toasty." There is no reason to comprehend a God that is at odds with himself: "tell me you're crazy maybe then I'll understand." God, however, refuses to come to his own defense: he's got his "9 iron in the back seat just in case." In the face of evil and God's neglect, Amos again implies that there may be a feminine corrective, this time on biblical terms. She quotes Proverbs 31:1: "Give not thy strength unto women nor thy ways to that which destroyeth kings." Turn the word of God back on God.

The reader should watch the video Amos created for "God." It begins in a Jewish synagogue. Amos is prostrate as rats crawl over her body, yet she handles them with pleasure. We see Jewish men putting on the tefillin—two small boxes with straps, one intended to be worn around the head and the other around an arm. The tefillin, which is of biblical origin (Deut. 6:5–8), includes a handwritten text, composed by a scribe, that consists of four passages, two from Exodus and two from Deuteronomy. Enveloping oneself in this way is the first mitzvah on the way to a young man's bar mitzvah. Thus, we are at prayer. Then the scene cuts for an instant (one could easily miss it) to a drug addict binding his arm as he prepares for the needle. The two events are thus implied to be equivalent. Next we move from rats to a Pentecostal service where snakes are being handled; Amos is herself part of the congregation. Back to rats. We appear now to be in India, first observing the feet of a man, and then moving to his bowl of food as rats envelop him. The music is jarring, grating. This is God.

Amos's song "Bliss" falls under the heading "Epistemology," and under the subheading "Origin and Destiny of Individual Souls." That knowledge is here connected with the origin and destiny of individual souls indicates that Amos's understanding of knowledge includes a belief in a prerational, a-rational, or irrational realm that hovers in the background of the intelligible world. "Bliss" is also a song about transgression, which is for Amos the locus of human freedom and the starting point to a proper understanding of the self. In other words, Amos reverses the orthodox understanding of the Fall as the locus of original sin. The song starts with a declaration: "Father, I killed my monkey." Now, the orthodox belief is that eating from the fruit of the Tree of Knowing Good and Evil led Adam and Eve to be banished from the Garden of Eden and is responsible for the deep spiritual wound suffered by all humans since. We are in the grips of our animal nature because the connection between the divine and human has been severed. Amos, however, rejects such a notion. Speaking of her monkey, she continues: "I let it out to / taste the sweet of spring / wonder if I will wander out / test my tether to / see if I'm still free / from you." The emancipated monkey both wonders and wanders. Mind and body are free. Ecstasy is the fruit of freedom achieved through disobedience. "Steady as it comes / right down / to you / I've said it all / so maybe we're a Bliss / of another kind." How curiously similar this is to Matthews's and Coldplay's evolutionary schemes.

Her emphasis on the body leads Amos to explore the orbit of science: "Lately, I'm into circuitry." Indeed, science and spirit form a strange alliance: "And I wonder if / you can bilocate is that / what I taste / your supernova juice / you know it's true I'm part of you." The term *bilocate* refers to a supernatural act by which one thing appears in two places simultaneously, the projection of one's spirit to another location keeping the body where it is. How the possibility of bilocation is meant to shed light on the effort to bring body and spirit together is not clear. Perhaps Amos is saying that under the old dispensation the body is captive. We are not free to indulge our passions. The act of liberation would require a new way of looking at the body, indulging it, but this is not the work of the body alone. The spirit must be involved. "Supernova juice" may be Amos's way of suggesting that we must tap into creative and destructive forces that allow for a new beginning (nova) that will transcend (super) the old one. A supernova, after all, occurs when a massive dying star (a so-called white dwarf) finally collapses because of the accretion of matter from a neighboring star, leaving behind either a neutron star or a black hole—or in any case, a new beginning.

We arrive at "Way Down," a song that falls under "Subconscious and Altered States," a subcategory of "Psychology." We are not done with souls. Nor are we done with the idea of a supernova. Amos speculates here that she is the "afterglow" (a reference to the light emanating from the Big Bang?) because "I'm with a band you know" (valance band? conduction band? the band structure?) Remember Amos's first band. We are in search of a new form of energy, sings Amos. Look who shows up for dinner. "Yes I am the anchorman / dining here with Son of Sam / hear too much to chat of on the way down." This discovery is juxtaposed with a great star. "Gonna meet a great, big star / gonna drive his great, big car / gonna have it all here on the way down." In the CD booklet some songs are printed against a black background, Amos appearing in bright colors (predominantly white), while other songs are printed against a white background, with Amos appearing in darker colors (and sometimes not at all).

We now come to what is arguably the climax of the album, "Crucify," the song that launched Amos's career and still defines her. Here we move from the cosmic Father to the earthly Son. Amos is like Dave Matthews, simultaneously repulsed by, attracted to, and fascinated by the crucifixion. According to her, we harbor a propensity to self-slaughter. We engineer events in ways that give credibility to our self-loathing. We poison our marriages, professions, and friendships. Our malignity is not a consequence of love's absence. Our hate harbors all of the virtues of erotic love. We are jealous, easily spurned, possessive, willing to give ourselves wholly to another—not as an act of charity but rather because we expect the same from them. We willingly take our lives when the demand for unconditional love is not met. Our death reminds the living of their failures—their failures to give wholly of themselves. Unconditional love demands unconditional love back. The thought that the living will spend the rest of their days with the memory of their all-too-conditional love makes the taste of death sweet. How worthy can we be in the face of he who gave his life for the world? His sacrifice now demands the greatest sacrifice from us—that we live wholly for him and not for ourselves. This goes by the name of love. The murder-suicide that is the crucifixion conquers the living—subdues them at the same time that they are spurred to demand the same unconditional love from others in the name of God. As God's viceroys, there are no limits to the demands of a limitless and infinite love. Hate thine enemies as thou hateth thyself.

"Crucify" speaks to all of these dilemmas, paradoxes, and contradictions. This song is not about emancipation but the trappings of a teaching that breeds, or so Amos thinks, destruction and self-destruction: "Every finger in the room is pointing at me / I wanna spit in their faces." Amos is possessed by the opinions of those she purports to hate: "then I get afraid what that could bring." Under these conditions Amos looks for "a savior in these dirty streets / Looking for a savior beneath these dirty sheets / I've been raising up my hands / Drive another nail in / just what GOD needs / one more victim." The deepest pleasures give no satisfaction, and Amos loathes her own self-pity. Her quest is an erotic desire for transcendence, a new birth: "I got a bowling ball in my stomach / I got a desert in my mouth / figures that my COURAGE would choose to sell out now." She is prior to conception, filled by preconceptions. She cannot give expression to her conception. Is the Immaculate Conception a thought? The first thought? The word? Answers are not forthcoming. Suffering is. "Why do we crucify ourselves / every day I crucify myself / nothing I do is good enough for you / Crucify myself / every day I crucify myself / and my HEART is sick of being in chains." Is love or eros at odds with itself, at once desiring freedom but lusting for dominion? "Got a kick for a dog beggin' for LOVE / I gotta have my suffering / so that I can have my cross / I know a cat named Easter / he says will you ever learn / you're just an empty cage girl if you kill the bird." Amos has "enough GUILT to start my own religion." The capitalized words belong to Amos.

As we saw in *Fight Club*, sex and possession is a theme that plays itself out in "Mary," a song that falls under the heading "Social Problems and Social Sciences" and the subheading "Abuse of the Earth." (In considering this track, note that Tori's first name, before she changed it, was Myra.) The song begins by working with stereotypes, uniting masculine mastery and feminine surrender: "Everybody wants something from you / Everybody wants a piece of Mary / Lush valley all dressed in green / just ripe for the picking / god I want to get you out of here." The song is usually taken as a statement on the way men look at and abuse women: "Growing up isn't fun / they tore your dress / and stole your ribbons / They see you cry / They lick their lips." However, in "Cooling" (*To Venus and Back*) we find the singer-protagonist projecting the same violent, erotic fantasies on the Virgin Mary. Is the singer-protagonist male or female? "But do I hate what she is / or do I want to be her / and don't we love something fresh / anything new, virgin." On the same album, "Lust" speaks of a woman's desire for a "prankster / and lust in the marriage bed." And in "Cruel" (*from the choir hotel*) Amos acknowledges that she "can be cruel," but she also says, "I don't know why." Amos, too, struggles against a masculine self.

In passing, we should note that "Snow Cherries from France" speaks of customs, etiquette, and folklore, "Silent All These Years" of linguistics and phonology, "Winter" of astronomy, "Professional Widow" of animals and spiders. There are intimate, personal songs that explain the scars on her body and soul and thereby reveal some of the reasons for Amos's rebellion. Under "Medicine and Health, Miscarriage" we find the song "Playboy Mommy." "Me and a Gun" is a heartwrenching tale about Amos's experience of rape; wonder is born of pain. Amos displays glimpses of painful wisdom in "Spark," a song she puts under the category "Natural Sciences" and the subheading "Philosophy and Theory." "Spark" portrays a woman who is "addicted to nicotine patches." The addiction masks a fear. "She's afraid of the light in the dark." Satan? The narcotic leads the protagonist to think lavish thoughts. A religion of darkness breeds extremes. "She's convinced she could hold back a glacier," that she controls life and death. "But she couldn't keep Baby alive (I'm getting old) / doubting if there's a woman in there somewhere."

Amos dismisses the idea of salvation as it is typically presented. Our task, rather, is to embrace the eternal return of the same. "You say you don't want it again and again." But you must accept it. "You say you don't want it / this circus we're in / but you don't you don't really mean it / you don't you don't really mean it." Perfection fails us. "If the Divine master plan is perfection / (swing low) / maybe next I'll give Judas a try / (swing low sweet chariot) / Trusting my soul to the ice cream assassin." The traitor (or the accomplice Judas?) is not the enemy (cf. "Professional Widow"—"everywhere a Judas as far as you can see / beautiful angel"). And yet Amos's own fortitude is brought into question: "How may fates turn around in the overtime / Ballerinas that have fins that you'll never find / you thought that you were the bomb / yeah well so did I / Say you don't want it / Say you don't want it / Say you don't want it again and again." Once again Amos turns to the darkness.

Amos is at odds with herself insofar as she cannot bear the weight of the eternal return of the same. She has a different salvation to contemplate. Thus do we arrive at "Precious Things," the first song on the album listed under "Collective Biography." Amos starts by trying to flee from the past: "So I ran faster / but it caught me here / yes my loyalties turned / like my ankle / in the seventh grade / running after BILLY / running after the rain." She tries to unshackle herself from possessions that possess her: "*These precious things / Let them Bleed / Let them*

Wash away / these precious things let them break / their hold on me"
(the italics are Amos's). But release alone will not suffice. What
is needed is active transgression. The Judas-like God justifies
her own Judas-like proclivities. Amos dies and resurrects. Her
rebirth brings forth justice, which here appears almost indistin-
guishable from revenge: "He said you're really an ugly girl /
but I like the way you play / and I died / but thanked him / can you
believe that / sick, sick, holding on to his picture / dressing up
everyday / I wanna smash the faces of those beautiful BOYS /
those christian boys / so you can make me c*m / that doesn't
make you Jesus." What is true of and for boys is no less true of
and for girls: "I remember yes / in my peach party dress / no
one dared / no one cared / to tell me where the pretty girls are
/ those demigods / with their NINE-INCH nails / and little
fascist panties / tucked inside the heart / of every nice girl."
The problem of patriarchy, then, is really the problem of human
nature. Matriarchy doesn't seem like a workable alternative.

original sexuality

Tales of a Librarian is an excellent primer for what I take to be
Amos's finest albums, *Scarlet's Walk* (2002) and *The Beekeeper*
(2005). These are stunning creations, arresting, beautiful, compelling—lyrically and musically. They are also provocatively
cryptic. *Scarlet's Walk* is an aural journey through America's
past. Neil Gaiman's *American Gods* hovers in the background
and surfaces in clever and unexpected ways. We have a song devoted to "Wednesday," for example, who in Gaiman's novel is
the incarnation of the god Odin. And in the strangely scientific
"Carbon," Amos calls for Neil: "Get me Neil on the line / No

I can't hold / have him read." Amos maps a journey through America just as Gaiman does in *American Gods*. And Jungian ideas and terms permeate both his understanding of the mystical and Amos's songs.

In *Scarlet's Walk* Amos neither vacillates nor ponders. Rather, she forthrightly appropriates the powers of the God-Christ and makes them her own. In "A Sorta Fairytale" the Word is now Amos's: "For me to break your bread / for me to take your word / I had to steal it." "Pancake" takes aim at both Christians and Cartesians, both of whom, Amos supposes, decided to "rewrite the law / segregate the mind / From body, from soul." The Promised Land is not God's paradise: "Oh, Zion please / remove your glove / + dispel every /trace / Of His spoken word / That has lodged / In my vortex."

In "Crazy," mania replaces religion. The euphoric wildness that makes a man go to the cross is replaced by emancipated sexuality. Call this the Jesus complex. "So I let Crazy take a spin / Then I let Crazy settle in / Kicked off my shoes / Shut reason out / He said 'first let's just unzip your religion down' / Found that I / I craved it all." Amos silences the nagging voice of reason. In "Don't Make Me Come to Vegas" we see her returning to the primordial light, to the "jester and a joker / and a dealer of men / they called him the prince / Prince of blackjacks and / of women and of anything / that slipped into his hands." Is she singing about Jesus or Satan? Or are they the same person? Amos's retelling of their encounter in the desert provides a clue to her thinking: "'And the Ranches and the mustangs' /and the way you said / 'You can have all this, / except for me—you see / Lady Luck is my mistress / and you'll have to play / second to her wish.'" Thus is the place of

Christ and the Devil's encounter removed from the desert to an infamous whorehouse.

"Don't make me come to Vegas" is followed by the song "Sweet Sangria." Whose blood are we drinking? The concluding song, "Mrs. Jesus," turns Jesus into a woman. In the spirit of Dan Brown, we learn that "the Gospel changes / meaning / If you follow John or / Paul / and could you ever / Let it be / the Mary of it all / and even as I'm / Climbing up the stairs." (If you are interested in further clues, consider this passage in light of songs devoted to the painter Marc Chagall, "Toast" in *The Beekeeper,* and the bonus track "Garlands." Chagall has a few things to show us about the Ark/Arch.)

We are ready for a new beginning. Amos says that *The Beekeeper* mirrors a cultural landscape of America. But appearances can be deceiving. *The Beekeeper* is organized around the theme of the "garden," and when Amos took *The Beekeeper* on the road she named the tour "Original Sinsuality." More than a cultural landscape of America, then, the album is really Amos's Genesis. In other words, we need a new genesis to go with our contemporary apocalypse.

The twelfth song of the album bears the title of the tour; here is the key lyric: "There was a garden / in the beginning / Before the fall / Before Genesis." If the garden predates Genesis, then it also predates the biblical God. Returning to the primordial garden would be coincident with a return to the primordial darkness. So what was "at the beginning"? In "Original Sinsuality" we learn that "There was a tree there / A tree of knowledge / Sophia would insist / You must eat of this." I cannot say if omitting "of good and evil" is deliberate, but if we are speaking of a time prior to God and thus prior to Satan, then the garden must also be prior to good and evil. Other signs also reveal that a reinterpretation of Genesis is underway. Wisdom, or "Sophia," insists on eating the apple, not Satan. Wisdom is prior to knowledge, though it seems that knowledge is necessary to wisdom, which does not make the two identical. The implications are enormous. Whence the original wisdom? Amos operates under the assumption (which she shares with Carl Jung) that there is an unconscious reality independent of but connected to us. We are not our own makers.

Amos goes back to the beginning because she is intent on supplanting the original Genesis. And this requires that she help us overcome the fear instilled by the orthodox or pedestrian reading of Genesis. In Amos's primordial garden, the wise quest for knowledge is not punished by death. One is not banished for seeking knowledge. Freedom is worthy of God's wrath insofar as it secures our emancipation from the wrathful God. The effort to liberate ourselves from tyranny and to make sense of the world is not a sin: "Original Sin? / No I don't think so," she sings. How does Amos justify her less-than-orthodox reading of Genesis? To answer that question, we need to take a detour through the biblical Genesis in order to show that the event we are taught to call a Fall is a complex tale about the antagonistic relationship between eros and logos, the latter understood both as the Greek "reason" and the biblical "Word" (cf. John 1). For, as we have seen, Amos is intent on recasting eros: "I've asked myself, Is there a way to reach an orgasm and keep your spirituality intact?"

None of what follows is original: the suggestions I make here about the meaning of the first three chapters of Genesis have been around for a very long time. First, God set out to create humankind (the Hebrew *adam*, which does not specify sex, later placed alongside *adama*, the Hebrew word for soil) in "his image" (Everett Fox translation). This image of God is both male and female—we are not yet at man and woman. In the text, there is a tension between the singular and the plural: "In the image of God did he create it, male and female he created them." One could argue that the original image is androgynous, composed of male and female parts; their plurality need not be of individual males and females. (The speech by Aristophanes in Plato's *Symposium* makes a case for the original human as male and female, severed by a vengeful deity. Original androgyny is at the heart of other creation myths as well.) God blesses the human thing and says: be fruitful and multiply. There is a command in place that sanctions the union of male and female.

Note that the story as it unfolds in Genesis 1 is mechanical and abstract. The author provides us with a sequence that is not temporal but divided into stasis (days 1–3) and motion (4–6). Genesis 2 provides another account of the creation through the eyes of named creatures. Here God acquires a name, YHWH. Scholars argue that Genesis 2 does not flow from Genesis 1; it might have been inserted later, they claim, and Genesis as a whole should be regarded as a disorganized compilation of various genesis myths. There is evidence to suggest otherwise, however. The first Genesis is generalized; the creation takes place in a rhythm and pattern. The second Genesis is particularized. Not only does God get a name, YHWH, but he also brings "each [living thing of the field and every fowl of the heavens] to the human, to see what he would call it; and whatever the human called it as a living being, that became its name." The named God teaches the human how to name, i.e., teaches him language.

The human names all his fellow creatures, but still "there could be found no helper corresponding to him." So "YHWH, God, caused a deep slumber to fall upon the human so that he slept, he took one of his ribs and closed up the flesh in its place." While the human is unconscious, "YHWH, God, built the rib that he had taken from the human into a woman, and brought her to the human." It is God, then, that seeks a helper for the human. Yet the human, not God, lays a claim on her—a claim that may not correspond to God's intent. God is silent. "The human said; This-time, she-is-it! Bone from my bones, flesh from my flesh! She shall be called Woman, *Isha*, for from Man, *Ish*, she was taken." How the human came to know of the events that transpired during his sleep is not stated. If God's anesthetic did its job, the human may be making unwarranted assumptions. Note, too, that woman is brought out of the unconscious. This is Jung before Jung.

Man is *made* but woman is *built*. The latter verb suggests that woman comes from the materials of nature already on hand. And if we say that Genesis 2 is an elaboration on the first creation story, we should wonder why the building of the woman takes place after the making of the human. Could it be that woman is the culmination of creation? After all, she gives birth and is thus equipped to create in ways men are not. That she is built implies a sophistication (the derivation from *sophia* intended) lacking in the human qua human. There is another cryptic suggestion that elevates woman. After the human lays claim to the woman, we hear echoes of the commandment to be fruitful. Someone says, we do not know who: "Therefore a man leaves his father and his mother and clings to his wife, and they become one flesh."

That primacy is given to woman becomes clearer as the story unfolds: "Now the two of them, the human and his wife, were nude, yet they were not ashamed." Note that we are not yet speaking of Adam. He has not acquired a name. Neither has the woman, whom we later call Eve. The two are unashamed. In keeping with Amos's allusions, could we say that the first couple is prepubescent? They are old enough to understand the command. They have logos. But eros may be too powerful for logos. Genesis may be a story about the need for logos to guide eros without depriving *eros* of its proper "erotic" power. "Philosophy" literally means "love of wisdom." "Philo-sophia" is erotic. From shamelessness, a condition in which we are not aware of sexual differentiation, the woman, not the man, confronts logos.

The nature of wisdom, however, is still in question. Intelligence or cleverness may be some part of wisdom, but it falls decisively short of accounting for all of what we mean by wisdom. A phallic creature with a forked tongue is described as being "more shrewd than all the living things of the field that YHWH, God, had made." God the Creator is clever, too: "It said to the woman: Even though God said: You are not to eat from any of the trees in the Garden . . . !" The three dots indicate that the sentence is incomplete, the exclamation perhaps indicating excitement. Note the woman's initiative and her aggression. She does not defer to the snake. It is curious that she should interrupt the serpent when we know that God's command or demand was made of the human prior (2:16) to the emergence of woman (2:22–23). Woman only knows of this prohibition at second- or third-hand. The Word is once or twice removed. In the original, "YHWH, God, commanded concerning the human, saying: From every (other) tree of the garden you may eat, yes, eat, but not from the Tree of the Knowing of Good and Evil—you are not to eat from it, for on the day you eat from it, you must die, yes, die."

The Tree of the Knowing of Good and Evil is planted in the "Land of-Pleasure." It is "desirable to look at." The Tree of the Knowing of Good and Evil is near the "Tree of Life," which, like all trees in the Garden, is also "desirable to look at and good to eat." The surroundings and circumstances are understandably confusing for our coming-of-age protagonists. The Garden is erotic through and through, and at its center is a prohibition against *logos*! The commandment not to eat of the Tree of the Knowing of Good and Evil emerges in the context of pleasure, and pleasure is so easily confused with good. Do we need reason to make the distinction? We are constituted in ways that prevent us from conflating the good with pleasure and the bad with pain. Working hard and enduring pains has its rewards. Correspondingly, indulgence, though initially pleasurable, often leads to pain. Pleasure does not satiate. Remember *Fight Club*. God can hardly be said to have provided clear instructions to his creations. Our confusion stems from the very constitution of the universe and the purposes of its Creator.

Back to Genesis 2. The woman interrupts and then speaks directly to the snake. "The woman said to the snake: From the fruit of the (other) trees in the garden we [the proverbial we] may eat, but from the fruit of the tree that is in the midst of the garden, God has said: You are not to eat from it and you are not to touch it, lest you die." Woman thereby amends the original commandment. God's word is altered. The snake responds: "Die, you will not die! Rather, God knows that on the day that you eat from it, your eyes will be opened and you will become like gods, knowing good and evil." Pride is aroused. Then the woman sees that the "tree was good for eating and that it was a delight to the eyes, and the tree was desirable to contemplate" (cf. Gen. 1). The woman ingests and digests. The Word is made flesh. Adam, who to this point in the drama has been conspicuous by his absence, now makes his passive appearance. "She took from its fruit and ate, and gave also to her husband beside her, and he ate." Eyes opened, they "knew then that they were nude." Here begins shamefulness.

Amos has reasons for transforming original sin into original sensuality. The remainder of the story provides more support for Amos's reading of Genesis as a story about eros and logos. The snake is punished. YHWH, God, puts "enmity between you and the woman, between your seed and her seed." Why is there enmity between sperm and egg? The woman is punished by multiplying "your pain (from) your pregnancy, with pains shall you bear children." Is pregnancy a consequence of the fall? The delight, the desire the woman felt, and the thoughts evoked now all "fall" under male jurisdiction. If the woman's punishment is subjection to the male, does that mean the original human condition was one in which the woman is sovereign over the male? "Toward your husband will be your lust, yet he will rule over you." The woman is then given a name. "The human called his wife's name: *Havva,* Life-giver! For she became the mother of all the living." Woman becomes mother.

Knowledge, taste, delight, desire, dominion, subjection, lust, husband, wife, mother, father, family, the perpetual flux between love and lust, the tension between knowledge and desire, good and pleasure, evil and pain, the perennial battle between the sexes . . . is the story not clear enough? Male loses his own sovereignty—over the earth. "Damned be the soil on your account, with painstaking labor shall you eat from it, all the days of your life. Thorn and sting-brush let it spring up for you, when you (seek to) eat the plants of the field." Man returns to the dust. This is not said of Eve (though she too will die), perhaps to indicate her powers of creation and procreation. The first reference to knowledge at the start of Genesis 4 is clearly and unequivocally a reference to sex. Eve gives birth to a son. God acknowledges, "the human has become like one of us, in knowing good and evil." God has rivals. The "winged-sphinxes and the flashing, ever-turning sword" now "watch over the way to the Tree of Life." In search for freedom the humans find subjugation, but this time to the forces of nature.

the dark lord

The Garden of Eden is the Land of Pleasure. It is populated by various trees, including the Tree of the Knowing of Good and Evil and the Tree of Life. Does our pursuit and indulgence of pleasures contribute to or detract from life? Is there a hierarchy of pleasures, and is that hierarchy known by way of commandment, experience, or reason? Why is the world—and why are we—created in such a way that the pursuit of natural pleasures deceives us or detracts from the pursuit of the good? Why are some pleasures good and some pleasures bad? What does it mean to know? Do we know the world and ourselves through contemplation or through experience? Could it be that knowledge is of two kinds, and that the two are not necessarily harmonious or mutually supportive? Is mind at odds with body? Would true wisdom consist of the marriage of bodily and spiritual knowledge?

We search for answers because we are creatures of speech. But naming is an abstraction. It gives us a false sense of dominion over the things we name. Such is the human's presumption, and woman pays the steepest price for it. What then is the status of language, and what is its relationship to the universe of things? What is the problem with logos or reason? God commands the human to be fruitful and multiply. When Adam and Eve fulfill the commandment, God punishes them. Is the so-called Fall a story of premature sex, of sex outside the boundaries of the law? If so, then the story of the Fall is not about sex per se. Do the various punishments meted out by God show that the price of freedom is labor? If so, would this constitute a punishment or a gift? I enjoy the fruit of my labor but do not enjoy the labor itself. We come to pleasure by way of pain. These questions are hardly exhaustive. But they do reveal that Amos is thinking and singing about preoccupations, dilemmas, confusions, hopes, fears, wants, and desires that are intrinsic to the human experience.

"Original Sinsuality" concludes with Amos's own fall into the darkness: "Yaldaboath /Saklas /I'm calling you /Samael / You are not alone / I say / You are not alone / In your Darkness / You are not alone / Baby / You are not alone." Gnostics believe that Sophia created a universe that challenges the original authority of God. She does so without a male counterpart. From the second act of creation comes a demiurge (craftsman or artisan) called Yaldaboath who declares herself God, with no being or power superior to hers. Is Amos comparing Yaldaboath to YHWH?

The conflation of good and evil deprives Amos of the capacity to see beyond power relations. For her, one power is supplanted by another possessing the same loathsome weapons. This is a democratic propensity animated by the principles of freedom and equality. Democracy deprives us of hierarchy—that is, deprives us of a natural order that is not egalitarian. We are moral creatures who judge and discriminate. Even toleration represents a judgment about the perniciousness of judgment. Toleration discriminates between the tolerant and the intolerant. Toleration condemns the intolerant as immoral at the same time that it claims that moral questions are for the individual alone, immune to the judgments of others.

Amos's solution to the oppression of morality and hierarchy eradicates the past, embraces nihilism, locates demonic powers in the no-thing, and seeks salvation in the revelatory experience of song and performance. But the concert ends, the crowd leaves the arena, and we all return to ourselves, yearning for another such moment. We grow contemptuous of the mundane present, and transgression by extremity becomes the norm. We erode the democratic conditions that make possible the very emancipation we seek, we sacrifice the social to the individual, but then in reaction we seek community, compassion, and fellow-feeling. We hate our hate but cannot quite shed our hate because we cannot shed ourselves. Oblivion. Annihilation. Hope for a Phoenix rising. But from whence, from what, from whom? Perhaps Amos gets the silence she seeks. That is the silence of despair.

A New Genesis
(Conclusions)

Language is the main instrument of man's
refusal to accept the world as it is. Without
refusal, without the unceasing generation by
the mind of "counter-worlds" . . . we would
turn forever on the treadmill of the present.
. . . Ours is the ability, the need, to gainsay or
"un-say" the world, to image and speak it otherwise. In that capacity in its biological and social evolution, may lie some of the clues to the
question of the origins of human speech and
the multiplicity of tongues. It is not, perhaps, "a
theory of information" that will serve us best in
trying to clarify the nature of language, but a
"theory of misinformation."

— George Steiner

Nothing is not about nothing. In the desire to erase our history, ourselves, and our responsibility we find a variety of noble longings, even as the process may undermine the satisfactions of those longings. The impetus to distinguish ourselves from what has been, to discover ourselves as more than the accretions of an inheritance, provides intimations of a soul that we hope is sheltered from the burdens of Time. We need not conclude that this flight of the imagination is itself nihilism, the cowardly and desperate failure to accept life on its own terms, as Nietzsche would have it. Even that most prescient German philosopher asserts that "[w]hat is done out of love always takes place beyond good and evil." We erase because we want to create anew. The impetus to do so is animated by the prospects of a new beauty and a new love. The apocalypse is as much about the passing as it is about the inauguration of a new era.

We could say, then, that the quest for nothing is not for nothing. We seek renewal. But that renewal must take place in the context of what is given. We do not, like gods, create ex nihilo. Whatever form we wish to make depends on the matter we have to work with. There is no simple "at the beginning," at least not for us. For this reason we find evolutionists, creationists, partisans of Intelligent Design virulently at odds with one another. There will always remain a gap in our understanding of the beginning. The beginning is always an inference. While I do not wish to denigrate the important and revealing attempts to rethink ourselves back to the start, there may be another route available to us that can harness both the impetus to self-erasure and the hope for a new beginning. Scientists, philosophers, theologians, all who speak a language may want to ponder whether contemporary battles may have more to do with Genesis 2 than Genesis 1.

Genesis 2 represents a new beginning. It retells Genesis 1 by emphasizing the importance of names and naming in contrast to the impersonal and formulaic account in the preceding chapter. God acquires a name, YHWH. And the human proceeds to name the creatures before him, exercising the power of language over the creation. In this chapter God discovers that it was "not good" for the human to be alone. The human too discovers a deficiency, namely, that among the creation there is no helper or sustainer corresponding to himself. Feeling and discerning an insufficiency indicates that we are not whole. We seem to know ourselves by what we lack. This is only half the story, however. The Genesis chapter on names and naming is simultaneously devoted to the divine and human capacity for negation. In naming we give meaning to a creature, draw it into mind and language, and in the process of describing it provide intelligibility and comprehension that would not be possible in the absence of words. Naming and being are not identical but they are inextricably linked. The ability to affirm that something "is" also permits us to negate its very being. But in so doing have we really made something into nothing? For to say something is not is to say that something is. There is much to learn about our contemporary naysaying.

Today we witness the full flowering of negation. America's own emergence as a product of will against the Void provides fertile ground for it, after all. This is an odd way of seeing ourselves and our polity. We live in an age of radical and violent affirmations, an age of black-and-white, divisiveness, virulence. But all this merely exposes the common fear we feel because of the vulnerability of our very claims "to be." The academy, furthermore, nurtures this citizenry of negation. "Essentialism" is tyrannical and imperial, we are told. What "is" is nothing but a construction, a fabrication, an artifice. The world is what we make it. Gender is a construction. Morality is a construction. But the artifact is not as believable as an artifact alone. We are something before we try to be something else. So what are we to do in the age of willful constructions? The very premise of deconstruction precludes any answer that might violate our radical freedom.

Deconstruction is only possible once we believe that everything is merely constructed. There is nothing genuine to claim. This flatters our presumption that we are gods, beings without restraint. But then what can we claim as our own, once everything has been deconstructed? Nothing. Deconstruction dissolves everything it touches. There is no text. There is no world. There is no us. There is no me. Thinking becomes "critical." It is not happenstance that the champion of deconstruction, Jacques Derrida, ended up writing a famous essay on the mystical foundations of the law. In the twilight of his life Derrida gave himself over to a dark, chaotic god.

To be sure, artifice is human and thus "natural" for us. Human grandeur is expressed through it and because of it. So is depravity. And herein lies the rub. The distinction between the noble and the base is more than a function of human artifice. As the artists discussed in this book wittingly or unwittingly reveal, we cannot get past the distinction between good and evil—even if we choose defiantly to affirm that we are beyond good and evil. Even nihilism, despite itself, affirms an order of being. Take this book as a tentative and less than adequate illustration of the manner in which even our greatest and most popular negaters can't shake a lingering sense that we are more than mere negation. The question of our age is not as Hamlet posed it: "To be or not to be?" We are. And we will cease to be. What does it mean to be and live in between? That is the question.

Bibliographic Essay

"Reading is stealing."
—various honest folks

pay homage to that time before we were all original. I cannot claim any thoughts as distinctly my own. My frame of reference is provided by the great books of Western civilization, the much-maligned canon. My ruminations on popular culture stem from twenty some years of wrestling with Greek tragedies and comedies, Homer's epics, Plato's cryptic dialogues, Aristotle's subtle treatises, the magisterial accomplishments of St. Augustine and St. Thomas Aquinas (the precursors to Protestant theology), Luther and Calvin. By my dim lights, I've pondered the Enlightenment, the likes of Bacon, Descartes, and Newton, the political philosophy of Hobbes, Locke, Hume, and Adam Smith, the rejoinders of Burke and Mary Wollstonecraft. Nietzsche and Heidegger presciently articulate the contours of our modern world. (Contemporary political theory I find less compelling.) There is no telling how much I imported from these authors into my own mind. The familiarity is such that I am no longer sure where my mind ends and theirs begins. It is harder still to determine whether my appropriation does justice to them.

All of the above smacks of pride. So let me make it clear that I could not have accessed the canon without many guides. I will not name my teachers for fear of indicting them. They know who they are. Several important essays and books have also helped to shape my thinking on popular culture. In particular, for me the Book of Genesis burst into life after reading Ronna Burger's "Male and Female Created He Them: Some Platonic Reflections on Genesis 1–3" in *Nature, Woman, and the Art of Politics*, ed. Eduardo A. Velásquez (Lanham, MD: Rowman and Littlefield, 2000), 1–18. A colleague subsequently introduced me to Phyllis Trible's *God and the Rhetoric of Sexuality* (Philadelphia: Fortress Press, 1978). Everett Fox and Robert Alter's translations of Genesis provided an entry to the text, given my own glaring language deficiencies.

I wrote a dissertation at the University of Chicago on the American Scottish founder James Wilson. There I began to explore the relationship between natural rights theory and the Scottish philosophy of sensibility. Without Michael Zuckert's writings I would have failed to understand the philosophical and theological sources of the American regime. Joseph Cropsey's *Polity and Economy: An Interpretation of the Principles of Adam Smith* (Westport, CT: Greenwood Press, 1977) first alerted me to the importance of Adam Smith as a modern thinker. But not until I wrestled with Charles Griswold's *Adam Smith and the Virtues of Enlightenment* (New York: Cambridge University Press, 1999) did I come to terms with the importance of sense and imagination in modern political thought. The chapter on *Copenhagen* could not have been written in the absence of Griswold's study of Smith's "impartial spectator."

Regarding the larger story of the Enlightenment and its relationship to nihilism, I am in Michael Gillespie's debt. *Nihilism Before Nietzsche* (Chicago: University of Chicago Press, 1994) opened to view that the Nominalist God is beyond good and evil. As to the character of nihilism itself Stanley Rosen's *Nihilism: A Philosophical Essay* (South Bend, IN: St. Augustine's Press, 2000 [repr.]) is indispensable. Since first picking up this work about six years ago I have taken it upon myself to read all things Rosen. I suspect that I have more debts to him than I could possibly acknowledge here. George Steiner's *Grammars of Creation* (New Haven, CT: Yale University Press, 2001) and *Real Presences* (Chicago: University of Chicago Press, 1989) helped me understand the virtue of pregnant silences, purposeful omissions, and fruitful negations. *Real Presences* also gave me an example of good literary analysis and helped me understand the metaphysical allure of contemporary culture.

The prospects of telling a story through stories emerged for me as I wrote "'Where the Wild Things Are': Re-Creation, Fall, Re and In ourrection in Chuck Palahniuk's *Fight Club*," in *Love and Friendship: Rethinking Politics and Affection in Modern Times*, ed. Eduardo A. Velásquez (Lanham, MD: Lexington Books, 2003), 575–616. The experience of writing that essay made it evident to me that the highfalutin speculations of philosophers and theologians do find their way into contemporary cultural artifacts. How is difficult to say. Few will read William of Occham, but plenty will watch and read *Fight Club*. In writing about popular culture I drew inspiration from my fellow political theorists Paul Cantor, Peter Lawler, and Mary Nichols. We are out to do different things. Yet their ability to engage popular culture seriously without having to draw from various incarnations of Marx's critique of capitalism and consumer culture, or psychoanalytic theories about the use of relative power, opened the door to the kind of engagement I have tried to provide here. Roger Ebert's review of *Fight Club* (the film) shows how easy it is to dismiss artifacts of pop culture that do violence to our sensibilities. Let us not make his mistake. (See www.suntimes. com/ebert/ebertreviews/1999/10/101502.)

Tidal waves don't beg forgiveness
"CRASHED" and on their way
Father he enjoyed collisions; others walked away
A snowflake falls in May.
And the doors are open now as the bells are ringing out
Cause the man of the hour is taking his final bow
Goodbye for now.

from Pearl Jam, "Man of the Hour"

Acknowledgments

A concern for the reputations and careers of various colleagues prevents me from acknowledging their support. They know who they are. Thank you. Three friends and interlocutors—Marshall Zeringue, Andrew Grant-Thomas, and Rafe Major—whose reputations cannot be affected saw this process through from beginning to end. I thank them for their kindness and fidelity. Without generous funding from the Earhart Foundation this book would not have seen the light of day.

To my students I owe a debt that I try to repay in this book. Many of the artifacts examined here first came to my attention because a student thought that our study of political philosophy shed light on them. Though taking a different form, and no doubt lacking the genius of a Plato or Nietzsche, popular, cultural artifacts continue an enduring conversation about our nature and place in the universe. We are too quick to dismiss pop culture. Socrates followed his *daemon* by asking interlocutors about their opinions; from there he tried to ascend to a plane of intelligibility that transcends mere opinion. The privilege of sharing this Socratic task with my students changed the course of my life: as student, writer, teacher, and mentor. I am the better because of them. There are too many students to thank, so I must extend my apologies to those whose names do not appear here. Kari Christoffersen and Michael Wagoner shaped this book in numerous ways, including its structure. The arrangement of chapters and sections is *entirely* theirs. Becky LeMoine proofread the manuscript before it landed in Jeremy Beer's lap. This book is less confused that it would have otherwise been because of Jeremy's careful and meticulous criticisms and encouragements.

This is an intimate book, borne of a personal and (at least for me) titanic struggle to come to terms with my own nature and the extent to which it might point beyond itself. Whether I *know* how to live with my doubt and self-doubt, in a universe replete with answers and simultaneously devoid of them, is a question that only a full life and death can answer. It will be for others to answer if there was any consequence to my being here. Throughout this ongoing existential struggle Andrea kept me connected to this life and to its many joys, carried me through dark times, and shared two children with me. Together, they brought me out of self-indulgence and helped me cultivate those simple, humane habits that give life meaning. No philosophic response to nihilism is complete. This is the great lesson I take from this book as it stares back at me.

Index

Abolition of Man, The (Lewis), 17

Adam, 27, 128, 144

aesthetics, morals and, xix, xx

agnosticism, 21

Alger, Horatio, 6

allometry, 24–25

America: Christianity in, xv; cultural landscape in, 136–37; Descartes, René and, 3; Enlightenment in, xv–xx, xxv; popular culture of, xiv; Protestantism in, xv–xvi; science and religion in, xiv; secular vs. religious in, ix

American Chopper, xiii

American Gods (Gaiman), x, 134–35

American Idol, xiii

American IV (Johnny Cash), 74

Amnesty International, 123

Amos, Tori, x, xi, xxiv–xxv:

Beekeeper, The, 125, 134, 136–37; *Boys for Pele,* 122–23; Christianity and, xxiv–xxv, 121–22; crucifixion and, 130–31; Dark Prince and, xxv, 122–23, 143–45; eros and logos and, 140–42; feminine and masculine and, xxiv–xxv, 123–24, 131–32; Gaiman, Neil and, 126, 134–35; Genesis, reinterpretation of and, xxv, 137–43; Gnostic Gospels and, xxiv, xxv, 121; God, assault on of, 126–27; *Little Earthquakes,* 125; mania and religion and, 135; Mary Magdalene and, xxiv–xxv, 121–22; nihilism and, 145; original sin and, 141–42; salvation and, 133; *Scarlet's Walk,* 125, 134–36; science and, 128–29; sexuality, original and, 134–42; *Tales of a Librarian*, 125–34; *Tori Amos: piece by piece* (Amos and Powers), 121–24; *To Venus and Back*, 125, 132

"Amsterdam" (Coldplay), 68

analogy, science and, 24

Anansi Boys (Gaiman), x, 126

antirationalism, 10

Apollo, 123

Apprentice, The, xiii

Aquinas, St. Thomas, xv, 28

Archimedean point, xvii

Aristophanes, 138

Aristotle, 11, 17–18, 28

Art: meaning of, xx; philosophy and, xx; science and, 23

Ashlee Simpson Show, The, xiii

atheism, 5, 21

atomic bomb, creation of, xxi, 35–36, 43–46, 54–55

Atwood, Margaret, x

Augustine, St., xv, 28

"Autobiography of Eve" (Twain), 99

Bachelor, The, xiii

Bachelorette, The, xiii

Bacon, Francis, 50

Baudot, Émile, 69

Beekeeper, The (Tori Amos), 125, 134: American cultural landscape and, 136–37; "Garlands," 136; "Original Sinsuality," 136–37, 144–45; "Toast," 136

Before These Crowded Streets (Dave Matthews), 89–92: "Don't Drink the Water," 92; "Last Stop," 91–92; "Pantala Naga Pampa," 90; "Rapunzel," 90–91; "Spoon," 92

being: knowledge and, 89–90; naming and, 149

Berryman, Guy, 58. *See also* Coldplay

Bible, xviii

Big Brother, xii

"Big Eyed Fish" (Dave Matthews), 82–83, 84

Big Loser, The, xii

Big Love, xii

Birth of Tragedy (Nietzsche), 123

Black Sabbath, xi

"Bliss" (Tori Amos), 127–29

Blunt, James, xi

Bohr, Christian, 55

Bohr, Margrethe, 41, 42–45, 46–50, 50–51, 55

Bohr, Niels, xxi, 32, 33, 34–36, 46–50: common sense and, 41; complementarity and, 34; empiricism of, 41; mathematics and, 38–41, 51; science and, 43; topography and, 40–41

Boys for Pele (Tori Amos), 122–23

brain, science of. *See* neuroscience

Britney and Kevin, xiii

Brown, Dan, xxiv, 121

Buckland, Jonny, 58. *See also* Coldplay

Busta Rhymes, xi

Busted Stuff (Dave Matthews): "Bartender," 96; "Big Eyed Fish," 82–83, 84; "Digging a Ditch," 96; "Grace is Gone,"

96; "Grey Street," 95; "Where
Are You Going," 95

Calvin, John, xvi
Camus, Albert, 87
Carnegie, Dale, 6
Carnivale, xii
Cash, Johnny, xi, 74
Catholicism: faith and reason
    and, 10; Protestantism vs., 27
Champion, Will, 58. *See also*
    Coldplay
Chapman, Tracy, vi
Chicago Sun-Times, 100
"Choir" (Tori Amos), 132
Christianity, xi: in America, xv;
    Amos, Tori and, 121–22; *Co-
    penhagen* (Frayn) and, 55; patri-
    archal, xxiv–xxv; Protestant,
    xv–xvi, 10; self and, xxiii; *see
    also* religion
"Christmas Song" (Dave Mat-
    thews), 88–89
"City of God" (Meirelles and
    Lund), 28
"Clocks" (Coldplay), 65–66
Coldplay, x, 94: birthing metaphor
    and, 66–67, Enlightenment
    and, 66; evolution and, 64,
    128; flesh made word and,
    69–72; God, biblical and,
    62–63; homelessness and,
    61–63; human and machine
    and, 71–72; love, science of
    and, 60–65; love and, xxii;
    nature and, xxii; nihilism and,
    70, 72; *Parachutes*, 58, 61; popu-
    larity of, 57; *Rush of Blood to*

the Head, A, and, 60–63; soul,
    search for and, 70; suicide and,
    67; time and, 65–68; *x and y*
    and, 60, 61, 69–74
complementarity, xxi–xxii, 33,
    34, 47
Confusion (Stephenson), x
conversations, science and, 36
"Cooling" (Tori Amos), 132
Copenhagen (Frayn), 64, 72: Chris-
    tianity and, 55; complementar-
    ity and, xxi–xxii, 33, 34; draft
    one of, 38–41; draft three of,
    46–50; draft two of, 41–46;
    God and, 55; Heaven and,
    51–52; knowledge of ignorance
    and, 38, 49; mathematics and,
    36, 38–41, 51; metaphysics
    and, xxii; morality and, xxii;
    Nazi atomic bomb program
    and, 35–36, 43–44, 54–55;
    quantum ethics and, xxii, 33,
    39, 42, 51–54; reductionism,
    materialistic and, xxii; science
    and politics and, 32; science
    fiction of, 34–38; uncertainty
    and, xxi–xxii, 33, 34, 40
"Crash" (Dave Matthews), 80–83:
    "Cry Freedom," 81; "Proudest
    Monkey," 81–82, 83, 84; "So
    Much to Say," 80–81
"Crazy" (Tori Amos), 135–36
Crucifixion: Amos, Tori and,
    130–31; fascination with, xi;
    Fight Club (Palahniuk) and,
    xxiv; Matthews, Dave and,
    47, 78
"Crucify" (Tori Amos), 130–31

"Cry Freedom" (Dave Matthews), 81

Culter, Frederick, 26

culture: American popular, xiv; of modernity, 57–58; will and, 13–14

Dark Prince, xxv, 122–23

Darwin, Charles, xxi, 20–23, 97

Darwinism, 4, 5

Dave Matthews Band. *See* Matthews, Dave

Da Vinci Code, The (Brown), xxiv, 121, 124

"Daylight" (Coldplay), 66

Deadwood, xii

Death Wish, 100

Declaration of Independence, xviii, 31–32

Delgado, José Manuel Rodriguez, 15–16, 23

demonic: Matthews, Dave and, xxiii

Derrida, Jacques, 150

Descartes, René, xvi, xix, 4, 50: America and, 3; doubt and, 15; dualism and, 11, 13

determinism, cultural, 16

Devil, Matthews, Dave and, xxiii, 77, 96–97

Devils and Dust (Bruce Springsteen), xi

Dictionary of Nobel Laureates, The, 12

Dionysus, 14, 91, 123

Discourse on the Method of Rightly Conducting One's Reason in the Search for Truth in the Sciences (Descartes), xvi

DMX, xi

dogma, xvii

"Don't Drink the Water" (Dave Matthews), 92

"Don't make me come to Vegas" (Tori Amos), 136

"Don't Panic" (Coldplay), 58

"Dreamed I Killed God" (Dave Matthews), 92–93

dualism: Descartes, René and, 4; *I Am Charlotte Simmons* (Wolfe) and, 11–14, 16–19; mind vs. body and, 4

Durden, Tyler, xxiv

Earth First, 123

Ebert, Roger, 99–100, 101

Ecce Homo (Nietzsche), 5, 26

Emerson, Ralph Waldo, 6

empiricism, science and, 41

Enlightenment, x: American, xv–xx, xxv; Coldplay and, 66; darkness of, xxvi; Declaration of Independence and, 31–32; gender differences and, xxvi; nihilism and, xxv; Protestantism and, xvii–xix; science of, xiv, xvii, xxv, 79; self and nature and, xvii; theology of, xiv, xvii, xxv

Erhard, Wener, 100

eros: battle for, xxv–xxvi; *Fight Club* (Palahniuk) and, 110–11, 112; logos and, 140–42; *see also* love

Eternal Sunshine of the Spotless Mind (Kaufman), 107

ethics. *See* quantum ethics

Eucharist, 89

Evanescence, xi

Eve, xxiv, 128, 144

Everyday (Dave Mathews): "The Space Between," 93–94

"Everything's Not Lost" (Coldplay), 60

evil: good and, xi–xii; good vs., xviii–xix, xxiii, 111–17

evolution, 20–23: Coldplay and, 64, 128; Matthews, Dave and, 82–83, 128

Extinction Level Event (Busta Rhymes), xi

Extreme Makeover, xii

faith: mathematics and, 40; philosophy and, 28; reason and, 10, 15, 27–29; science and, 14–19

Fallen (Evanescence), xi

Fallen (Sarah MacLachlan), xi

Fall of Man, 78, 113, 128

Feirelles, Fernando, 28

feminine: Amos, Tori and, xxiv–xxv; in *Fight Club* (Palahniuk), xxiv; masculine and, xiii, 83–85, 113–17, 123–24, 131–32, 138–40; sacred and profane and, xxiv

Fight Club (movie): popularity of, 101–2; reviews of, 99–101

Fight Club (Palahniuk), xxv, 141: commercial republicanism and, 102; creation, story of and, xxiv, 105; crucifixion and, xxiv; eros and, 110–11, 112; eroticized violence in,

101, 104; eternal life and, 110, 112–13; feminine and masculine in, 113–17; God and, 102, 109, 113–17; good vs. evil in, 111–17; ironies in, 107–8; liberation, themes of in, 101; life as death and, 103–11; masculinity and femininity and, xxiv; narrative of, 104–11; nihilism and, 102–3; original sin and, 110, 111; pain and pleasure in, 117; perfection, pursuit of and, xxiv; rebirth and, 102–3; silence, yearning for and, xxiii–xxiv; soul, understanding and, 112; synopsis of, 103–4; transcendence, yearning for and, xxiii–xxiv; wholeness and, 105–6, 108, 111

Fincher, David, 99, 101

"fix you" (Coldplay), 67, 71–72

Flaubert, Gustave, 8–9

Flesh, Word and, 17, 36

Forbes magazine, 3

Frayn, Michael: complementarity and, 33, 34; knowledge of ignorance and, 38; metaphysics and, xxii; morality and, xxii; Nazi atomic bomb program and, 35–36; quantum ethics and, xxii, 33, 39; reductionism, materialistic and, xxii; science and politics and, 32; science fiction of, 34–38; uncertainty and complementarity and, xxi–xxii, 33, 34; *see also Copenhagen* (Frayn)

freedom, quantum mechanics and, 33
Freud, Sigmund, 17
Freudianism, 6
from the choir hotel (Tori Amos): "Choir," 132

Gaiman, Neil, x, 126, 134–35
Galileo Galilei, xix, 32
Garden of Eden, xxiv, 128, 143
"Garlands" (Tori Amos), 136
Genesis, 113: Amos, Tori reinterpretation of, xxv, 137–43
"ghost in the machine, the," 4, 13
Gnostic Gospels, xxiv, xxv, 121
Gnosticism, 86
God: Amos, Tori and, 126; Coldplay and, 62–63; *Copenhagen* (Frayn) and, 55; creation and, xx; darkness of, xxii; death of, x, 5–7; as demonic, xxiii; the Father, xxiv, 113–14; feminine and masculine and, 113–17, 138–40; *Fight Club* (Palahniuk) and, 102, 109, 113–17; insufficiency of, 62–63; loathing of, xi; Matthews, Dave and, 92–93; morality and, xv; the Mother, 114–15; nature and, xvi; Nature's, xviii; reason and, xv, xvii; the Son, 117; will and, xvii
"God Put a Smile Upon Your Face" (Coldplay), 62–63
God's Son (NAS), xi
"God" (Tori Amos), 126–27
"Gravedigger" (Dave Matthews), 85

Greatest Salesman in the World, The (Mandino), 6
Greek philosophy, xv, 17–18
"Grey Street" (Dave Matthews), 95

Hahn, Otto, 43–44
Hamlet, xxii
Handmaid's Tale, The (Atwood), x
Hanging Out with Dream King: Conversations with Neil Gaiman (Amos), 126
HBO, xii
Heaven, 51–52, 80, 112
Hegel, Georg Wilhelm Friedrich, 17
Heisenberg, Werner, xxi, 33, 34–36, 46–50: as Cartesian, 41; mathematics and, 38–41; Nazi atomic bomb program and, 35–36, 43–46, 54–55; quantum ethics and, xxii, 39, 51–54; uncertainty and, 34, 43
Heisenberg's War: The Secret History of the German Bomb (Powers), 35
"Hello Again" (Dave Matthews), 77
"High Speed" (Coldplay), 59
Hilton, Paris, xiii
History of the Peloponnesian War (Thucydides), 36
Hitler, Adolf, 35
Hobbes, Thomas, 31–32, 50, 102
Hollywood, 100, 101
Hooking Up (Wolfe), 3
Houellebecq, Michel, 8
How to Win Friends and Influence People (Carnegie), 6
human, machine and, 71–72

I Am Charlotte Simmons (Wolfe):
conservatives and, 9–10;
critics and, 9–10; Darwin,
Charles and, 20–23; faith and
reason and, 27–29; *Madame
Bovary* (Flaubert) and, 8–9;
mind, body, and culture in,
11–14; mind-body dualism
and, 16–19; nihilism and, 26;
philosophy vs. poetry and,
7–11; religion and, 25–29; science and, 14–19, 20–23, 23–25;
scientific faith and, 14–19; self
and, xxi, 10, 22–23; will and,
13–14
ignorance, knowledge of, 38, 49
imagination, nihilism and,
148–51
individuality, time and, 65
"In My Place" (Coldplay), 62
Institute for Theoretical Physics, 34
Intelligent Design, 148
Iron Maiden, xi
irrationalism, 29
It's Dark and Hell is Hot (DMX), xi

Jefferson, Thomas, 31–32
Jesus Christ: Matthews, Dave
and, 88–89; as personal, xvii,
xviii; suffering, xi
Johansen, Jojo, 17
John the Baptist, St., 55
Judas Priest, xi
Jung, Carl, x, 137, 139

Kant, Immanuel, 5
Kaufman, Charlie, 107

Kierkegaard, Soren, 87
Knowledge: being and, 89–90;
dangers of, 50; of ignorance,
38, 49
Kuhn, Thomas, 31

Laguna Beach: The Real *Orange
County*, xiii
"Last Stop" (Dave Matthews),
91–92
Laws of Nature, xviii, 31–32
Leipzig, University of, Germany,
34
Lewis, C. S., 17
Little Earthquakes (Tori Amos), 125
Locke, John, 31–32, 50
logic, logos and, xxvi
logos, xxvi: eros and, 140–42;
logic and, xxvi; mythos and,
xxvi; poesis and, xix, xxvi
Lost, ix
love: Coldplay and, xxii; Mat-
thews, Dave and, xxiii; science
of, 60–65; *see also* eros
Luck and Pluck (Alger), 6
Lund, Katiá, 28
Luther, Martin, xvi

Machiavelli, Niccolo, 50, 91
machine: human and, 71–72;
nature and, 73
MacLachlan, Sarah, xi
Madame Bovary (Flaubert), 8–9
"Man Comes Around, The"
(Johnny Cash), 74
Mandino, Og, 6
mania: religion and, 135; thought
and, 80

Man in Full, A (Wolfe), 11
Manor House, The, xiii
Manson, Marilyn, xi
Marla, xxiv
Martin, Apple, xi, 60
Martin, Chris, xi, 58, 60, 72. *See also* Coldplay
Martin, Moses, xi, 60
Marx, Karl, 50
Marxism, 6
Mary Magdalene, xxiv–xxv, 121–22
"Mary" (Tori Amos), 131–32
masculine: feminine and, 83–85, 113–17, 123–24, 131–32, 138–40; in *Fight Club* (Palahniuk), xxiv
materialism, 10, 80
mathematics, xviii: *Copenhagen* (Frayn) and, 36, 38–41, 51; faith and, 40
Matrix trilogy, ix, 124
Matthews, Dave, xi, 117: *Before These Crowded Streets,* 89–92; *Busted Stuff,* 84, 95–96; Christmas and, 88–95; *Crush,* 80–83, 84; crucifixion and, 47, 78; Devil and, xxiii, 47, 77, 96–97; evolution and, 82–83, 128; feminine and masculine and, 83–85; God, struggle against of, 47, 80–81, 92–93; Jesus Christ and, 88–89; knowledge and being and, 89–90; life as death and, 85–88; love and, xxiii; memory and, 78; nihilism and, xxiii; original sin and, 78, 81, 86; *Remember Two*

Things, 83–85, 87–88, 88–89; silence and, xxiii, 93; *Some Devil,* 85, 96–97; *Stand Up,* 77; suicide and, xxiii; *Under the Table and Dreaming,* 78–80; *see also* Dave Matthews; Matthews, Dave
"Me and Gun" (Tori Amos), 132
Mendel, Gregor Johann, 21
"message, a" (Coldplay), 74
Metallica, xi
metaphysics: Frayn, Michael and, xxii; science and, ix, xx, xxii–xxiii
Metaphysics (Aristotle), 17–18
"Minarets" (Dave Matthews), 84
modernity: culture of, 57–58; as project, 108; suicide and, 8
"Monkey Island," 23–24
morality: God and, xv; as theatrical and sentimental, xxii
morals, aesthetics and, xix, xx
Morrison, Van, xi
Munich, University of, 34
My Big Obnoxious Boss, xiii
mythos, logos and, xxvi

naming, being and, 149
Napalm Death, xi
NAS, xi
nature: Coldplay and, xxii; God and, xvi; laws of, xviii; machine and, 73; return to, xiii, xvi–xvii; science and, x, 79; self and, xvii; technology vs., 79; will and, 13–14
Nature's God, xviii, 31–32

neo-Platonism, 28

neuroscience: atheism, dogmatic and, 21; impact of, 3–5; philosophy and, 5; politics and, 6; religion and, 5; scientific method and, 23; self and, xxi, 10

New-Age spiritualism, 86

New Battlestar Galactica, ix

Newton, Isaac, xv, xix, 32, 34

Nietzsche, Friedrich, 21, 33, 92, 100, 123: atheism and, 87; Dionysus and, 91; God, death of and, 5–7; nihilism and, 26, 148; science, meaning of and, 57; will to power and, 8

nihilism: Amos, Tori and, 145; Coldplay and, 70, 72; Enlightenment and, xxv; *Fight Club* (Palahniuk) and, 102; *I Am Charlotte Simmons* (Wolfe) and, 26; imagination and, 148–51; Matthews, Dave and, xxiii; Nietzsche, Friedrich and, 148; quantum ethics and, 33; quantum physics and, 33; religion and, 102

Nominalism, xvi

Norton, Edward, 100

nuclear weapons, development of, xxi, 35–36, 43–46, 54–55

occult, xvii

"One Sweet World" (Dave Matthews), 83–84

original sin: Fall of Man and, 128; *Fight Club* (Palahniuk) and, 110, 111; Matthews, Dave and, 78, 86

"Original Sinsuality" (Tori Amos), 136–37, 144–45

Origin of Species, The (Darwin), 20–21

Oryx and Crake (Atwood), x

Osbornes, The, xiii

Palahniuk, Chuck, 99, 126: commercial republicanism and, 102; creation, story of and, xxiv, 105; crucifixion and, xxiv; *Fight Club* (Palahniuk) and, 103–11; God and, 109; nihilism and, 102–3; perfection, pursuit of and, xxiv, silence, yearning for and, xxiii–xxiv; transcendence, yearning for and, xxiii–xxiv; wholeness and, 105–6, 108, 111; *see also Fight Club* (Palahniuk)

Paltrow, Gwyneth, xi, 60

"Pancake" (Tori Amos), 135

"Pantala Naga Pampa" (Dave Matthews), 90

Parachutes (Coldplay), 58, 60, 61: "Don't Panic," 58; "Everything's Not Lost," 60; "High Speed," 59; "Shiver," 58; "Spies," 58–59, 64; "Trouble," 59; "We Never Change," 59–60

Pay the Devil (Van Morrison), xi

Peale, Norman Vincent, 6

philosophy: art and, xx; faith and, 28; Greek, xv; neuroscience and, 5; as pathology, 5

Physical Control of the Mind: Toward a Psychocivilized Society (Delgado), 15

Pimp My Ride, xii–xiii
Pitt, Brad, 100
Plato, 17, 28, 138
"Playboy Mommy" (Tori Amos), 132
poesis: logos and, xix, xxvi; self and, xxvi; techne and, xxvi
poetry, xxi: techne and, xxvi
politics: neuroscience and, 6; science and, 32; science of, 50
"Politik" (Coldplay), 61–62
Pollock, Jackson, xiv
Possessed, xi
Power of Positive Thinking, The (Peale), 6
Powers, Ann, 121
Powers, Thomas, 35
practice, theory and, 50
praxis, theory vs., 50
"Precious Things" (Tori Amos), 125, 133–34
"Professional Widow" (Tori Amos), 132, 133
Prometheus, xviii, 55
Promised Land, xi, 60
Protagoras, 32
Protestantism: American, xv–xvi; Catholicism vs., 27; Enlightenment, xvii–xix; faith and reason and, 10; reason and, 27
Protestant Reformation, 27, 29
"Proudest Monkey" (Dave Matthews), 81–82, 83, 84
Providence, xviii

quantum ethics, xxii, 33: *Copenhagen* (Frayn) and, xxi, 39, 42, 51–54; nihilism and, 33; skepticism and, 33; uncertainty and complementarity and, 47
quantum mechanics: conversations and, 36; Copenhagen interpretation of, xxi, 34; freedom and, 33; ignorance and knowledge and, 33, 38
quantum physics, xix, 33
Quat, Jerry, 26
Queen, ix
Queer Eye for the Straight Guy, xii
Quicksilver (Stephenson), x

"Rapunzel" (Dave Matthews), 90–91
rationalism, 5, 15
Raymond, St., 28
Raymond of Penafort, St., 28
reality, nature of, xii, xiii
reality television, xii–xiii
reason: faith and, 10, 15, 27–29; God and, xv, xvii; heart and, x; Protestantism and, 27; soul and, xvii
reductionism, xxii, 10, 11, 28
relativity, xix
religion: *I Am Charlotte Simmons* (Wolfe) and, 25–29; irrationalism and, 29; mania and, 135; neuroscience and, 5; nihilism and, 102; as pathology, 5; science and, xv, 25–26; *see also* Christianity
Remember Two Things (Dave Matthews), 83–85: "Christmas Song," 88–89; "Minarets," 84; "One Sweet World," 83–84;

"Satellite," 83; "Seek Up," 84–85, 87–88

Renaissance, 32

Return to Bedlam (James Blunt), xi

"Rhyme and Reason" (Dave Matthews), 79

Rhymes, Busta, xi

Ritchie, Nicole, xiii

Roth, Buster, 26

Rousseau, Jean-Jacques, 82

"Rush of Blood to the Head, A" (Coldplay), 67–68

Rush of Blood to the Head, A (Coldplay), 60–63; album cover of, 60–61; "Amsterdam," 68; "Clocks," 65–66; "Daylight," 66; "God Put a Smile Upon Your Face," 62–63; homelessness and, 61–63; "In My Place," 62; "Politik," 61–62; "Rush of Blood to the Head, A" 67–68; "Scientist, The" 63–65, 67; suicide and, 67; time and, 65–68; "Whisper, A" 66–67

salvation, xvi, 133

Sartre, Jean-Paul, 87

"Satellite" (Dave Matthews), 78–79, 83

Scarlet's Walk (Tori Amos), x, 125, 134–36: America's past and, 134; "Carbon," 134–35; "Crazy," 135–36; "Don't make me come to Vegas," 136; "Pancake," 135; "A Sorta Fairytale," 135; "Sweet Sangria," 136; "Wednesday," 134

science: allometry and, 24–25; Amos, Tori and, 128–29; analogy and, 24; art and, 23; of brain, 3–5; Coldplay and, 57–74; conversations and, 36; *Copenhagen* (Frayn) and, 31–55; empiricism and, 41; Enlightenment, xiv, xvii, xxv, 79; faith and, 14–19; *I Am Charlotte Simmons* (Wolfe) and, 3–29; as impersonal activity, 43; irrationalism and, 29; limitations of, x; of love, 60–65; Matthews, Dave and, 83–84; meaning of, 57; metaphysics and, ix, xx, xxii–xxiii; modernity, culture of and, 57–58; nature and, x, 79; observation and experience and, 31; of politics, 50; politics and, 32; religion and, xv, 25–26; scientific method and, 23; of self, xxi; skiing and, 40, 43–44; sociobiology, origins of and, 23–25; theology and, xxv; uncertainty and, 46–47

scientific method, xvi, 23

"Scientist, The" (Coldplay), x, 63–65, 67

Second Discourse (Rousseau), 82

secularism, 80

"Seek Up" (Dave Matthews), 84–85, 87–88

self: abolition of, 22–23; Christianity and, xxiii; *I Am Charlotte Simmons* (Wolfe) and, 22–23; nature and, xvii; neuroscience and, 10; poesis and, xxvi; science of, xxi

self-government, 6, 32
"Self-Reliance" (Emerson), 6
Shelley, Percy Bysshe, xxi
"Shiver" (Coldplay), 58
silence, xxiii
"Silent All These Years" (Tori
    Amos), 132
Simple Life, The, xiii
skepticism, 21, 33
skiing, science and, 40, 43–44
"Snow Cherries from France"
    (Tori Amos), 132
Society for Neuroscience, 5
sociobiology, 23–25
Socrates, 17–18, 21, 28, 29, 33
Some Devil (Dave Matthews), xi,
    xxiii, 47: "Gravedigger," 85;
    "Save Me," 96–97
"So Much to Say" (Dave Mat-
    thews), 80–81
Sophia, xxv, 137
Sopranos, The, xii
"Sorry, but Your Soul Just Died"
    (Wolfe), 3, 7, 8, 10, 26
"Sorta Fairytale, A" (Tori Amos),
    135
soul: Coldplay and, 70; death of,
    7; *Fight Club* (Palahniuk) and,
    112; reason and, xvii; rediscov-
    ery of, 10; search for, 70
"Space Between, The" (Dave
    Matthews), 93–94
"Spark" (Tori Amos), 132–33
"speed of sound" (Coldplay), x
"Spies" (Coldplay), 58–59, 64
"Spoon" (Dave Matthews), 92
Springsteen, Bruce, xi
Stand Up (Dave Matthews): "Hello

Again," 77
Starling, Victor Ransom, 11–13,
    15–16, 20, 22, 23
Steiner, George, 147
Stephenson, Neal, x
Street Disciple (NAS), xi
sublimation, 17
suicide: Coldplay and, 67; *Madame
    Bovary* (Flaubert) and, 8;
    Matthews, Dave and, xxiii;
    modernity and, 8
Survivor, xii
"Sweet Sangria" (Tori Amos), 136
Symposium (Plato), 138
System World (Stephenson), x

Tales of a Librarian (Tori Amos),
    125–34: "Bliss," 127–29; "Cru-
    cify," 130–31; feminine and
    masculine and, 131–32; "God,"
    126–27; God, assault on of,
    126–27; "Mary" and, 131–32;
    "Me and Gun," 132; order of
    songs in, 125–26; "Playboy
    Mommy," 132; "Precious
    Things," 125, 133–34; "Profes-
    sional Widow," 132, 133;
    "Silent All These Years," 132;
    "Snow Cherries from France,"
    132; "Spark," 132–33; "Tear in
    Your Hand," 125, 126; "Way
    Down," 129; "Winter," 132
"Tear in Your Hand" (Tori
    Amos), 125, 126
techne, poesis and, xxvi
technology, nature vs., 79
television: good and evil in,
    xi–xii; reality, xii–xiii

Tell, William, 66

"Telling Stories" (Tracy Chapman), vi

Temptation Island, xii

theology: Enlightenment, xiv, xvii, xxv; negative, xxii; science and, xxv

theory, practice and, 50

thinking, will and, xvi

Thomas Aquinas, St., xv, 28

Thorpe, Hoyt, 28

thought, mania and, 80

Thucydides, 36–37

"Til Kingdom Come" (Coldplay), 74

time: individuality and, 65; nature of, x

"Toast" (Tori Amos), 136

Tocqueville, Alexis de, 3

tolerance, 16

Tori Amos: piece by piece (Amos and Powers), 121 24

To Venus and Back (Tori Amos), 125: "Cooling," 132

Tree of Knowing Good and Evil, 128, 141, 143

Tree of Life, 141, 143

"Trouble" (Coldplay), 59

Twain, Mark, 77, 99, 121

uncertainty, xxi–xxii, 33, 34, 40, 43, 46–47

Under the Table and Dreaming (Dave Matthews), 78–80: "Rhyme and Reason," 79–80; "Satellite," 78–79; thought and mania and, 80; "What Would You Say," 78

Virgin Mary, xxiv–xxv, 132

Void, xiv, xix, 102, 109, 149

Wachowski, Larry, 124

Wagner, Richard, 77

"Way Down" (Tori Amos), 129

"Wednesday" (Tori Amos), 134

"We Never Change" (Coldplay), 59–60

"What Would You Say" (Dave Matthews), 78

"Where Are You Going" (Dave Matthews), 95

"Whisper, A" (Coldplay), 66–67

"white shadows" (Coldplay), 70–71

will: culture and, 13–14; God and, xvii; nature and, 13–14; power of, 87; salvation and, xvi; thinking and, xvi

William of Ockham, xv–xvi

Wilson, Edward O., 22, 23–25

"Winter" (Tori Amos), 132

Wolfe, Tom, 108: Darwin, Charles and, 20 23; faith and reason and, 10, 27–29; materialism and, 10; mind, body, and culture in, 11 14; mind-body dualism and, 16–19; as moral conservative, 26; neuroscience and, 3–5; nihilism and, 26; philosophy vs. poetry and, 7–11; reason and, 26; reductionism and, 10, 11, 28; religion and, 25–29; science and, 14–19, 20–23, 23–25; scientific faith and, 14–19; self, abolition of and, 22–23; self

and, xxi, 10; will and, 13–14;
see also I Am Charlotte Simmons
(Wolfe)
Word: flesh and, 17, 36; truth of,
xviii

"x and y" (Coldplay), x
x and y (Coldplay), 60, 61: album
cover of, 69; childhood, recovering and, 70–71; "fix you,"
67, 71–72; flesh made word
and, 69–72; human and ma-
chine and, 71–72; "message, a"
74; nihilism and, 72; "speed of
sound," 72–73; "Til Kingdom
Come," 74; "white shadows,"
70–71; "x and y," 72–73

YHWH, 138–42
Y Kant Amos Read, 125

About the Author

Eduardo Velásquez teaches political philosophy, science and the arts, literature, and popular culture at Washington and Lee University in Lexington, Virginia. He has taught or held residence at Lake Forest College, the University of Chicago, Haverford College, the University of Edinburgh, and Oxford University, among other institutions. He received his B.A. from the University of California at Santa Barbara and his M.A. and Ph.D. from the University of Chicago, all in political science. He is the editor of *Love and Friendship: Rethinking Politics and Affection in Modern Times* and *Nature, Woman, and the Art of Politics*.